EMINENT PITTSBURGHERS

Eminent Pittsburghers
Profiles of the City's
Founding Industrialists

William S. Dietrich II

TAYLOR TRADE PUBLISHING
Lanham • New York • Boulder • Toronto • Plymouth, UK

Published by Taylor Trade Publishing
An imprint of The Rowman & Littlefield Publishing Group, Inc.
4501 Forbes Boulevard, Suite 200, Lanham, Maryland 20706
http://www.rlpgtrade.com

Estover Road, Plymouth PL6 7PY, United Kingdom

Distributed by National Book Network

British Library Cataloguing in Publication Information Available

Library of Congress Cataloging-in-Publication Data
Dietrich, William S.
 Eminent Pittsburghers : profiles of the city's founding industrialists /
William S. Dietrich II.
 p. cm.
 ISBN 978-1-58979-607-2 (cloth : alk. paper) – ISBN 978-1-58979-613-3
(electronic)
 1. Industrialists–Pennsylvania–Pittsburgh–Biography. 2. Businessmen-
-Pennsylvania–Pittsburgh–Biography. 3. Pittsburgh (Pa.)–Biography.
4. Pittsburgh (Pa.)–Economic conditions. I. Title.
 HC108.P7D54 2011
 338.092'274886–dc22

 2011015794

∞™ The paper used in this publication meets the minimum require-
ments of American National Standard for Information Sciences—
Permanence of Paper for Printed Library Materials, ANSI/NISO
Z39.48-1992.

Printed in the United States of America

Dedicated to
Edwin V. Clarke, Jr.
Anne Dietrich Diemer

CONTENTS

1

A VERY SHORT HISTORY OF PITTSBURGH

FOR PITTSBURGH GEOGRAPHY AND GEOLOGY HAVE BEEN destiny. Geography comes first. Close upon the confluence of the Allegheny and Monongahela rivers one gets a sense of westward flowing waters, but a map of Western Pennsylvania shows the Allegheny flowing south and the Monongahela north, almost at right angles to the Ohio. A fourth river comes into play: the Potomac, which brings the coast of Virginia (allowing for some tough navigation) quite close to the Monongahela. Lastly—the mountains. The western slope of the Alleghenies lies some forty miles from the Point. From there it's a straight 1500-mile shot to the Rockies. Pittsburgh not only faces but opens the great heartland of America. Before the canals and railroads the Ohio and Mississippi river systems were the interstate highways of their day.

By the mid–eighteenth century (1751) there were three claimants to southwestern Pennsylvania: the French, the

"View of Pittsburgh and Allegheny." Lithograph by Otto Krens (c.1874). Courtesy of the Library of Congress

English, and the Indians. Geographically the French were in the strongest position. They had undisputed control over the two great waterways that drained the North American continent: the St. Lawrence and the Mississippi. They were weaker but still dominant in the Ohio valley. The best passage through the Alleghenies was up the Potomac to the Monongahela and then down the Ohio. Lucrative trade and rich soil were irresistible draws for the expanding English colonies.

It was Virginia's soldier aristocrats rather than William Penn's Quakers who first breathed life into southwestern Pennsylvania. In 1747 a group of prominent Virginians, including Lawrence Washington and, as a minor participant, his half-brother George, founded the Ohio Company. They applied to the English king for a grant of two hundred thousand acres. Soon after the royal grant was received the Ohio Company began to exploit its new lands. The French, under the firm hand of the Marquis du Quesne in Montreal, took decisive action. They established Fort Le Boeuf on French Creek within striking distance of the three rivers. Governor Robert Dinwiddie of Virginia (an Ohio Company investor) sent a young George Washington up to Le Boeuf to protest.

Outmanned and outgunned Washington protested and left, in December of 1753; it was round one to the French.

Responding with alacrity early in 1754, Dinwiddie sent an Ohio Company party to the forks to build Fort Prince George, the first English fort west of the Alleghenies. In April 1754, a French army of five hundred confronted the handful of men at the fort, which promptly surrendered. The French renamed it Fort Duquesne, over which the Fleur-de-lis was to fly for the next three years; round two to the French. Dinwiddie raised new forces and an advance party under George Washington pushed through to Fort Necessity fifty miles southeast of the fort. After one successful skirmish Washington was forced to surrender in July; round three to the French.

It was now obvious that the Ohio Company, even with the help of Virginia and Pennsylvania, was not going to drive the French Empire out of the Ohio Valley. General Edward Braddock was the first in a long line of unfortunate choices as British commanders in America. He assembled a force of 2200 regulars and colonials and, on July 9, 1755, marched them to a stunning defeat against an inferior force of French and Indians on the site of today's Edgar Thompson Works, ten miles from the Point. The loss was staggering—456 dead and 421 wounded; round four to the French. Things were not looking good for the English.

Fortunately for the American colonists the conflict in the Ohio Valley—our French and Indian War—was a small part of the global struggle between France and England known as the Seven Years War (1756–1763). It pitted England and Prussia and their indomitable leaders William Pitt the Elder and Frederick the Great against the rest of Europe. Pitt assumed full power in 1757 and arrogantly declared: "I can save this country and nobody else can." He was true to his word. The English fleet swept the French from the seas and destroyed France's colonial power in America, Africa, and India.

The American piece played out under General John Forbes who was assigned the retaking of Fort Duquesne. Forbes assembled an army of 6,000, including 2,000 regulars, 2,500 Pennsylvanians, and 1,500 Virginians. The force was overwhelming but the French still had some fight left in them. An impetuous Major James Grant rushed ahead with a detachment of 800 at a hill near today's courthouse. The French and their Indian allies defeated Grant in a smaller reprise of Braddock's Field. Grant's name does live on in Pittsburgh's own Champs Elysees: Grant Street. The capture of Fort Duquesne was anticlimactic. The French, weakened by serial defeats in Quebec and on Lake Erie, simply abandoned the fort; round five to the English in a TKO. Forbes wrote Pitt: "I have used the freedom of giving your name to Ft. Duquesne." Thus we became Pittsburgh with an official birthday in 1758.

There was an inevitability to the English triumph in America. Had there been no Pitt, had Braddock been a better general, the English triumph may have come sooner or later but it was destined to come. One word tells the story: population. The French, forced to defend a frontier running from Nova Scotia to the Gulf of Mexico, had a scant eighty thousand. The English colonies had a compact population of 1.25 million; it would double in twenty years. The force of numbers alone destined the English colonists to pop the cork at the Point and sweep the French, Spanish, and Indians back in an irresistible floodtide.

After the ratification of the Constitution in 1789, commerce and industry replaced politics as a story line in Pittsburgh history. But one final political chapter had yet to play out. In 1791 Congress adopted an excise tax upon whiskey. In Western Pennsylvania the tax bit especially hard. One in five farmers operated a still. Additionally, in the largely self-sufficient agricultural economy, cash was scarce while whiskey

was plentiful. The tax itself was not unreasonable. The rub came as the farmers sold their whiskey not for cash but bartered it. In short, they had a liquidity problem. The cry went up that the tax was unjust and the farmers would defy the newly formed national government. George Washington and the ever-energetic Alexander Hamilton responded with overwhelming force. Washington personally led thirteen thousand militiamen partway to Pittsburgh and Hamilton negotiated a settlement. It was a critical victory for the young republic.

Abundant natural resources, including wood, coal, limestone, and sand, along with flax and cotton, coupled with the mountain barrier to Eastern imports drove Pittsburgh to early self-sufficiency. The river network meant that raw materials could be shipped to Pittsburgh, aggregated through simple manufacturing, and then easily transshipped.

In the period from 1790 to 1810, arguably the most important industry in Pittsburgh was boat building. The rich forests of Western Pennsylvania and fast river transit landed the required materials at the perfect location at the head of the Ohio. Two principal types of boats were built in Pittsburgh. The flatboat was used exclusively for downriver running. Length varied from twenty to one hundred feet and width from twelve feet to twenty feet. Construction was simple; a pile of logs and a bucket of nails and you were good to go. Prices varied from a dollar to a dollar and fifty cents a foot. The average boat carried fifty tons. The journey to New Orleans was a one-way trip. Once there you sold the boat for the value of the lumber.

Keelboats were used for upriver hauls. Trips from New Orleans to the Point took four months. Downstream it was only four weeks. Lewis and Clark began their fabled trip to the Pacific in a Pittsburgh keelboat in 1803. That same year Pittsburgh built the 170-ton brig *Dean*, which sailed from Pittsburgh down the Mississippi and across the Atlantic to

Liverpool. And in 1811 Nicholas Roosevelt, a partner of Robert Fulton, launched the first steamboat on western waters. The *New Orleans* carried 450 tons and made the trip to Louisville in sixty-four hours. Soon steam spread to gristmills and iron rolling mills. By 1812 the local firm of Oliver and Evans was manufacturing steam engines.

Politically the region began to take shape when in 1788 Allegheny County was created from parts of Washington and Westmoreland counties. The city of Pittsburgh was incorporated in 1816. The merchant, Ebeneezer Denny, was named mayor. The best sign of the city's gradual transformation from a commercial to a manufacturing center was given by a visitor in 1818. He observed: "Dark dense smoke and a hovering cloud of vapor." It would get much worse over the next 125 years.

The period between the end of the War of 1812 (1814) and the outbreak of the Civil War (1861) saw a pronounced shift in Pittsburgh's economy from commerce to industry. Part of the shift resulted from several challenges to Pittsburgh's near monopoly on the western trade. As the population west of Pittsburgh surged, downriver cities such as Cincinnati, Louisville, and St. Louis began to challenge Pittsburgh as supply points near to the frontier. In 1825 the Erie Canal connected the Hudson River to Buffalo spurring the growth of Cleveland, Detroit, and Chicago. This was not trade that Pittsburgh lost—she never had it, but it did put a damper on future commercial growth. A far greater threat was the decision of the U.S. Congress to terminate the National Road (today's U.S. 40) at Wheeling on the Ohio, bypassing Pittsburgh. After its completion five thousand Conestoga wagons from Baltimore unloaded annually at Wheeling, West Virginia. For a while it looked like Wheeling might offer a strong challenge to Pittsburgh. But manufacturing momentum favored Pittsburgh and Wheeling eventually languished.

Many of Pittsburgh's industries required iron. The heart of its economy rested upon iron and later steel. Charles Dickens visited the city in 1842 and observed: "Pittsburgh is like Birmingham in England . . . and is famous for its iron works." Iron production began in the hinterlands closer to sources of wood for charcoal; adequate veins of iron ore were found in Fayette, Somerset, and Washington counties. Local foundries turned out simple shapes, nails, and farm implements, while supplying a host of machinery manufacturers.

Pittsburgh may claim in Samuel M. Kier (1813–1874) a multifaceted industrialist in canal boats, fire brick, medicines, and most importantly oil refining. When oil began to seep into his father's salt wells in Tarentum, Kier accepted the challenge of marketing the then-unwanted fluid. Illuminating oil replacing whale oil was the targeted market; smoke and odor made crude oil unacceptable. Kier rose to the challenge of refining by distilling the crude in a five-barrel still built at a site one hundred feet from today's U.S. Steel Building. Through Kier's inventive genius Pittsburgh, for a period before John D. Rockefeller's consolidation of the oil industry, was the refining center of the nation.

The Civil War gave great impetus to Pittsburgh's nascent industrial base. Pittsburgh rapidly became the arsenal of the Union. The Fort Pitt Foundry cast over three thousand cannon, including the world's largest at twenty inches. The cannon that armed the Union's first ironclad warship, the USS *Monitor*, was cast in Pittsburgh.

The Golden Age

The forty-year period from 1870 until 1910 marks Pittsburgh's golden age. Favorable geography, unique natural resources, and a superabundance of entrepreneurial talent lifted Pittsburgh to a position of national and international prominence never seen before or since. Pittsburgh's growth is a

story of heavy industry—more specifically, steel. Population statistics speak to Pittsburgh's dynamism during this period. The city's population grew from 86,076 to 533,905, or a 6.2-times increase. Allegheny County grew from 262,204 to 1,018,463, or a 3.9-times increase. The U.S. population increased from 38,000,000 to 92,000,000 for a 2.4-times increase. Pittsburgh grew at twice the national rate.

How did Pittsburgh become the steel capital of the world? First there was iron. Pig iron is the product of the smelting process: the reduction of iron ore in a blast furnace. It has a high carbon content and is less malleable than steel. From Colonial times until 1850 iron production was localized based on iron ore sources and ample forests for charcoal—the smelting fuel of choice. As the demand for iron production grew rapidly between 1840 and 1870, larger tracts of forestland were required to provide the required charcoal; deforestation was a problem. At first charcoal was replaced by anthracite (hard coal) produced in northeastern Pennsylvania, but by 1875 bituminous (soft) coal in the form of coke from southwestern Pennsylvania provided over 50 percent of blast furnace fuel. Coke is prepared when great heat is applied to coal kept out of direct contact with air; it is nearly pure carbon.

And now for the geology. The Connellsville coal seam is part of the famous Pittsburgh coal bed which extends throughout southwestern Pennsylvania. The Connellsville seam runs for sixty miles from Latrobe in the north to ten miles south of Uniontown in a south/southwest direction. Connellsville lies at its center. It varies between 2.5 to 3 miles across, and occupies 180 square miles, or 115,000 acres.

The seam itself was a generous eight to ten feet thick with an average overburden of sixty feet to one hundred and fifty feet. With coal that was almost free of slate and sulfur, the resultant coke was porous and hard, allowing for stability in the furnace stack. It was a near-perfect fuel.

Coal was transformed to coke in the Connellsville fields by means of beehive ovens, averaging seven feet high and twelve feet in diameter. They were cheap to build. During its prime production years from 1880 to 1935, the Connellsville region shipped 500 million tons of coke, requiring 770 million tons of metallurgical coal. At its peak, 39,000 beehive ovens produced over 20 million tons of coke annually. The direct and indirect wealth produced by this bounteous gift of nature far exceeded the value of all the gold and silver ever mined in the United States.

Of the three required elements of blast furnace burden, iron ore, coal, and limestone, Pittsburgh had the latter two. Economics dictated steel making in close proximity to the coal fields rather than the Lake Superior iron ore ranges—Michigan and Minnesota. Cheap coke and coal made possible the concentration of the steel industry. A one-half acre of Connellsville coal produced the fuel equivalent to two thousand acres of forestland.

In addition to its riches in coking coal, three interrelated factors destined Pittsburgh to be the nation's steel capital: the Bessemer process, the railroads, and Andrew Carnegie. The Bessemer steel-making process consisted of air blown through molten iron in a five-to-seven-ton egg-shaped Bessemer converter. It was the joint work of an Englishman, Henry Bessemer, and an American, William Kelly. The oxygen in the air decarbonized the iron, "converting" it to strong workable steel. The Bessemer process was widely adopted in the United States between 1865 and 1875. It made possible the mass production of steel. The iron industry soon became the steel industry. Fortunately Bessemer-driven mass production of steel coincided with an insatiable demand on the part of U.S. railroads for steel rails. Railroad trackage in the United States was a modest thirty thousand miles in 1860. It doubled by 1870 and increased eight-fold by 1900.

Into this confluence of mass production and mass market walked one of the most extraordinarily talented figures in American business history. Andrew Carnegie (1835–1919), after a meteoric rise at the Pennsylvania Railroad, left to attend to a host of business ventures he had financed while still employed by the railroad. His mentor, Thomas A. Scott, and the Pennsylvania Railroad president, J. Edgar Thompson, were coinvestors in most of these ventures. The Pennsylvania was invariably the major customer. In those days, conflict of interest was an alien concept.

In 1872 Carnegie organized a syndicate to construct a steel plant of one hundred thousand tons' capacity on a site in Braddock. Scott and Thompson were in from the start. The plant was named the Edgar Thompson Works. It was one of the first plants designed with Bessemer converters specifically to make rails—a single-purpose plant. Carnegie made an extraordinary hire in Captain Bill Jones, the best operating man in the business. In its first year of production the plant was profitable and was the lowest-cost producer of rails in the United States. Nobody could sell rails like Carnegie. He used his pricing power to telling effect. One can scarcely overestimate the importance of the railroads in American industrial history and in the growth of the steel industry. Until 1890 the railroads were pretty much the market. Not only rails, but locomotives, rail cars, bridges, and tunnels added to the tonnage. In the '70s and '80s, Pittsburgh was a hotbed of new steel startups. Two notable efforts at Homestead (1881) and Duquesne (1890) succumbed to Carnegie's sharp competitive thrusts and were absorbed into the larger company.

Carnegie didn't have it all his own way. Jones & Laughlin Steel dated from before 1855. It never attempted to meet Carnegie head-on in rails but sidestepped him by producing a variety of products, including shapes, nails, and bars. By the end of the century J & L produced 650,000 tons of steel and

went on to become the fourth-largest steel producer in the United States.

By 1900, fully integrated in both iron ore and coal, Carnegie Steel was the largest steel company in the country with three million tons of capacity. In 1901, J. P. Morgan consolidated the steel industry, combining Carnegie and seven other major companies into the giant U.S. Steel Company with a capitalization of $1.4 billion—the largest private company in the world. It controlled 60 percent of U.S. steel production with over 40 percent coming from the Carnegie properties. By 1910 Pittsburgh produced 25 million tons of steel, over 60 percent of the nation's total. It was the high-water mark for Pittsburgh's share of national steel production.

During the forty years between 1870 and 1910 Pittsburgh was a seething cauldron of entrepreneurial activity. Matching Carnegie in industrial prominence was the Mellon family. In 1870 Judge Thomas A. Mellon established a private bank, T. Mellon & Sons. He was soon joined by his third surviving son A. W. Mellon (1855–1937). Through financial acumen rivaling J. P. Morgan, he built the Mellon Bank into the thirteenth largest bank in the country. In 1889 he and his brother R. B. (1858–1933) financed the Pittsburgh Reduction Company, later Alcoa—for over one hundred years the largest aluminum company in the world. In 1900 the Mellons, along with nephew W. L. (1848–1949), founded the Gulf Oil Company. It eventually accounted for 40 percent of the family fortune and became one of the seven sister international oil companies. Mellon's fingers were everywhere. In addition to his three largest holdings, A. W. founded Koppers, Carborundum, Union Steel Company, Standard Steel, Pittsburgh Coal, McClintic-Marshall, and a host of other sizable companies.

George Westinghouse (1846–1914) moved to Pittsburgh from Schenectady, New York in 1873. Pittsburgh beckoned

because it was a rail hub with low steel costs and abundant metalworking talent. He patented his revolutionary air brake in 1869 and built Westinghouse Air Brake into a Fortune 500 company. As an inventor (371 patents), Westinghouse stands second only to Thomas A. Edison. In 1886 he founded the Westinghouse Electric Company—at its peak the thirteenth largest industrial company in the United States.

Henry Clay Frick (1849–1919) built a vast fortune on the mineral wealth of the Connellsville coal seam. Known as the coke king he was originally financed by Judge Mellon and became a close confidante of A. W. Mellon. In the '80s Frick needed money and Carnegie needed coke. Carnegie bought a controlling interest in the H. C. Frick Coke Company and Frick ran the entire Carnegie operation. Despite a final rupture it was a win/win relationship. Henry J. Heinz (1844–1919) founded the precursor of the H. J. Heinz Company in 1869. The Heinz Company was the odd man out as a branded consumer products company in a town totally dominated by heavy industry.

By 1970 Pittsburgh would have the distinction of being the third-largest corporate headquarters city in the United States. With but few exceptions all these companies or their antecedents were founded during the period between 1870 and 1910: Alcoa, Allegheny Ludlum, Blaw-Knox, Consolidation Coal, Copperweld Steel, Crucible Steel, Dravo, Fisher Scientific, Gulf Oil, Harbison Walker, H. J. Heinz, Jones & Laughlin, Joy Manufacturing, Koppers, Mellon National Bank, Mesta Machine, Mine Safety Appliance, National Steel, Pittsburgh Chemical, Pittsburgh National Bank, Pittsburgh Plate Glass, Pittsburgh Steel, Rockwell International, United Engineering and Foundry, United States Steel, Universal Cyclops, Westinghouse Air Brake, and Westinghouse Electric. With the exception of the two banks, Heinz, and a couple of light manufacturing companies, it was heavy industry all the way.

In only forty years the industrial growth of Pittsburgh was breathtaking. It was an era of unprecedented dynamic entrepreneurism. For those at or near the top of the heap it was a glorious time. For the vast majority it was a burden to be born. Most work in the mills was twelve hours a day, six and seven days a week. Enlightened employers such as Heinz and Westinghouse were the exception.

Two of the most violent strikes in U.S. labor history occurred during this period. The more famous of the two is the Homestead strike, compounded by Carnegie's malicious attempt to dodge all personal responsibility. The more violent of the two was the great railroad strike of 1877. In it over twenty were killed and property damage was over $5 million ($100 million in today's dollars). It was all for naught; unions were not to be a factor until the 1930s.

The Long Slide

During the golden age Pittsburgh had developed an industrial economy that was the envy of the world. The major enterprises that were launched drove the Pittsburgh economy to new heights for the next fifty years. So strong were these Pittsburgh corporations that they carried nearly the entire weight of the local economy. The entrepreneurial era of the golden age became the managerial era. Pittsburgh was a quintessential "company town." For both white and blue collar job seekers Pittsburgh had a host of good jobs. With the advent of Pittsburgh unionism in the late '30s Pittsburgh's blue collar jobs became even more desirable.

Unfortunately there was a downside to Pittsburgh's overspecialization in steel and heavy industry. Because the jobs were so attractive they drew potential entrepreneurs away from smaller businesses.

Population again tells the story. In 1930 the population of Pittsburgh peaked at 699,817. By 2000 it was 343,600—roughly

half. Some of this was out-migration to the county. But here the story is equally bleak. In 1938 Allegheny County had a population of 1,374,410 and in 2000 1,277,700. Between 1910 and 2000 the U.S. population increased by 3.1 times whereas Allegheny County lost 9 percent of its population. In 2000 Pittsburgh had the second oldest demographic profile of any U.S. metropolitan county save for Dade County, Florida.

Despite a static population, by midcentury good jobs in Pittsburgh's heavy industry manufacturing sector were still plentiful. Economic development was not a high priority. What was a high priority was Pittsburgh's environment. Pittsburgh exited World War II (1945) having given over the Point to a tangle of railroads and warehouses. Through a combination of the steel mills and the universal use of soft coal for home heating the sky was often pitch black at 9:00 a.m. If you think Beijing is bad today, you should have seen Pittsburgh in 1945. Despite a vital economy Pittsburgh was dying at its core and in danger of losing the head offices of the companies that made it great.

Two very different men formed a compact and a shared vision to put Pittsburgh back on track. David L. Lawrence (1889–1966), mayor of Pittsburgh from 1946 to 1959, was the foremost political figure this city ever produced. Richard King Mellon (1899–1970), the son of R. B. Mellon, was the chairman of Mellon National Bank and through his vast holdings was the natural leader of the Pittsburgh business establishment. With the able assistance of Wallace Richards and Arthur Van Buskirk, and through the instrument of the Allegheny Conference, they gave birth to what became known as the Pittsburgh Renaissance. Smoke control legislation was passed, the skies cleared, and the industrial jungle at the Point was razed and replaced with a park and several new office buildings. In a brief fifteen years the face of Pittsburgh changed dramatically.

Ironically the year Lawrence left office in 1959 saw the first serious rupture in Pittsburgh's industrial underpinnings. It came in the form of a crippling, 116-day industry-wide steel strike. It opened the door to the first major influx of imported steel. It was a problem that would eat away at the industry for the next forty years, eventually bankrupting twenty-nine steel companies. The Pittsburgh industrial behemoth hummed along very well into the 1970s, but beneath the surface the tectonic plates of fundamental economic change were grinding on. Pittsburgh-based steel companies were expanding capacity but not in Pittsburgh. Light sheet steel for appliances and automobiles was their most important market and it was best served from steel plants in the middle west.

In the late 1980s over 75 percent of the steel-making capacity near Pittsburgh was shuttered. Sprawling facilities running along the Monongahela and Ohio rivers toppled like tenpins: the Pittsburgh Steel plant in Monessen, U.S. Steel facilities in McKeesport, Duquesne, and Homestead, J & L Pittsburgh, and Aliquippa. Who is to blame for this tragedy? Everybody and nobody. The demise of the steel industry in Pittsburgh played out with the inevitability of a Greek tragedy. Our loss of jobs was a body blow such as no major American city had ever received, and worse was to come. For a while we consoled ourselves with the fact that Pittsburgh was the third-largest corporate headquarters city in the United States. The brawn may have gone elsewhere but the company brains remained in Pittsburgh. Sadly, over 75 percent of our major corporations in 1970 are no longer here today. To save ink it's easier to list those that are still here rather than those we lost: Allegheny Technologies, H. J. Heinz, Mine Safety Appliance, PNC, PPG, and U.S. Steel. We also have two Westinghouse spinouts: Wesco and Westinghouse Nuclear, and two new arrivals—Federated Investors and Dick's Sporting Goods. It's a short list.

A New Day

The worst is now behind us. Environmentally the city is in good shape. Our economy is more balanced than ever before. We can no longer be called a company town. Numerous opportunities in venture-backed startups and growing small businesses now often have more appeal than a slow rise up on the escalator of corporate hierarchy.

Three strong bell cows are leading us toward a technology-based future: Carnegie Mellon University, a top twenty-five AAU university, the University of Pittsburgh, with broad-based strength capped by the health sciences and a school of medicine ranking sixth in NIH funding, and the University of Pittsburgh Medical Center, now the largest academic medical center in the United States with $7 billion in revenues and over fifty thousand employees.

Like a Janis-headed creature we may look forward to a brighter future and, with great pride and a little nostalgia, look back to a time long ago when Pittsburgh forged the industrial might that made America the greatest nation in the world.

2

ANDREW CARNEGIE: THE BLACK AND THE WHITE

THE PHILOSOPHER HANNAH ARENDT HAS FAMOUSLY AND aptly termed the 1800s as the "over-busy" nineteenth century. During this "over-busy" century, nobody was "busier" than Andrew Carnegie. He cut a broad swath across the economic and philanthropic landscape of America unequaled ever since.

Means of Ascent

Carnegie was born in Dunfermline, Scotland in 1835. His parents, William and Margaret Morrison Carnegie, were both descended from long lines of Scottish political radicals and free thinkers. Their first child, Andrew, was born into modest but promising circumstances. Will Carnegie was a third-generation weaver; his trade was damask weaving, whereby intricate and elaborate patterns were woven into linen. Shortly after Andrew was born Will moved the family into larger quarters, bought new looms, and hired apprentices to accommodate

Andrew Carnegie. Courtesy of the Library of Congress

his expanding business. Andrew's simple ambition was to become a great weaver. His father was his first hero.

Unfortunately, the weaving trade and the modest economic underpinnings of the Carnegie family were directly in the crosshairs of the first stage of the industrial revolution: textiles. By 1835 there were 110,000 power looms in Great Britain. Will Carnegie believed his damask skills made him immune from the competition of the mass textile market. However, the invention of the Jacquard loom programmed by punch cards spelled the end of the elder Carnegie's economic utility. Every year brought a tightening of the economic vise

until in 1847 a defeated Will Carnegie told his son: "Andra I can get nae mair work." In 1848 the family, including Andrew's younger brother Tom, emigrated to America. They joined Margaret's sister in Pittsburgh.

The family settled on Pittsburgh's North Side, then known as Allegheny City. Will found only sporadic work and Margaret, always the driving force of the family, became the breadwinner by sewing shoes for their neighbor, Henry Phipps, for four dollars a week. Phipps's son, Henry, Jr., would later ride the tiger to great riches with Margaret's son. The wolf was at the Carnegie door as Margaret's $4.00 per week was short of providing the bare necessities of food and shelter. Andrew had to find work.

His first job as a bobbin boy at the Blackstock Cotton Mill paid $1.20 a week for a twelve-hour day, six days a week. In a few months a bobbin manufacturer gave young Carnegie a job at $2.00 a week. Through an introduction by his uncle he was taken on as a messenger boy with the Atlantic & Ohio Telegraph Company at $2.50 per week. This was his first big step and he knew it: "There was scarcely a minute in which I could not learn something. . . . I felt that my foot was on the ladder and that I was bound to climb." Several of his fellow couriers, including lifelong friends David McCargo, Henry Oliver, and Robert Pitcairn, came to future prominence.

While not out delivering messages Andy began to sit in for the telegraph operators and soon learned the trade. In 1851 he was promoted to full-time operator at a salary of $4.00 a week. As a manifestation of his extraordinary talent he was soon able to translate the telegraph clicks directly into words, reputedly only one of a handful throughout the industry who were able to do so. With his astounding telegraphy skills and his willingness to take on any available managerial duties, Andy's profile began to rise. This was not without design. As Carnegie himself once said, "The rising man must

do something exceptional, and beyond the range of his special department. He must attract attention."

And attract attention he did. He soon drew the notice of Tom Scott, the superintendent of the western division of the Pennsylvania Railroad. He joined Scott as his telegraph operator in 1853. One morning, only a few months on the job, he took bold action bordering on the reckless. A serious accident had logjammed a good portion of the western division. Scott could not be located. In direct disregard of standing orders, Carnegie sent out instructions under Scott's name rerouting several trains, and in short order unclogged the system. Scott was so pleased at Carnegie's boldness and initiative that he bragged about it to the president of the Pennsylvania Railroad, the formidable J. Edgar Thompson, calling Carnegie "his little white-haired Scottish devil." Carnegie, Scott (born 1820), and Thompson (born 1808) were linked by a common thread. They had absent or weak fathers, and they threw themselves into work as a substitute for family (all married late in life—Scott at 46, Carnegie at 51). They fit into father-son roles: Thompson for Scott and Scott for Carnegie; and all three were born speculators.

In the heady days, as the Pennsylvania Railroad became the largest industrial enterprise in America, the notion of "conflict of interest" was almost unknown. It was common practice for railroads' key insiders to invest in railroad suppliers and to buy up property in the path of new lines. It was a surefire way to make money. In 1856 Scott arranged for Carnegie to invest $500 in Adams Express, a package shipping company; he loaned him the $500. Several other "supplier" investments followed. The bell-ringer was the Woodruff Sleeping Car Company. For an investment of $250 (borrowing the rest), Carnegie ended up holding shares that generated $5,000 ($100,000 in today's dollars) in annual dividends in 1863. Years later Carnegie attempted to rewrite the Woodruff

story, claiming that Woodruff, "a farmer looking kind of man," brought the idea first to Carnegie, who then alerted Scott and Thompson to the opportunity. It was pure fiction.

In 1859 Scott was promoted to vice president of the Pennsylvania Railroad in Philadelphia. Despite Edgar Thompson's reservations about Carnegie's age (24), Scott named him superintendent of the western division in Pittsburgh at an annual salary of $1,500 per year. In ten short years he had advanced from bobbin boy at $62 a year to an executive position responsible for over one thousand employees. To top it off his income from outside investments dwarfed his now princely salary. How did he do it?

Fundamental to an understanding of Andrew Carnegie is recognition of his extraordinary talents. Set one on one against his peers, Rockefeller, Mellon, and Ford, you had to bet on Carnegie. Carnegie was spectacularly talented in numerous dimensions. He was highly intelligent and possessed a gritty pragmatism and street smarts; he was a consummate salesman, using charm and a Scottish brogue that he fell in and out of to suit the occasion like a slide trombone player. He was 5 feet 3 inches with tiny hands and feet. Requiring little sleep, he was a bundle of nervous energy. Today he would be diagnosed as hypomanic—a variant of manic-depressive conditions with all of the highs and none of the lows. And not least, he was a fearless risk taker. Like all great men he had a vision (steel), but in this case it came much later. For the first thirty-seven years of his life it was all about execution.

Deal Maker

Carnegie's first venture into the iron and steel business was quite inauspicious. In 1863 two skilled iron masters, Anthony and Andrew Kloman, approached Thomas Miller to request $1600 to expand their forge business. Miller, not having

the cash, brought in Henry Phipps, Jr. The Klomans and Phipps then combined forces to force out Miller, who turned to Carnegie to arbitrate. Carnegie elected rash action and agreed to back Miller to build a competing mill to drive the Klomans and Phipps out of business. There was one slight problem. Miller and Carnegie didn't know the iron business. "Cyclops Steel" could not produce an acceptable product. For Carnegie it was a disaster. Not only was it a money loser but Carnegie had friends in both companies. All fingers were pointed at Carnegie.

Demonstrating his consummate negotiating skills, he salvaged the situation, convincing the warring parties to merge. Carnegie brought together the considerable technical capabilities of the Klomans and the ample order book that he was able to provide through his railroad contacts. He bought out the disgruntled Miller and the newly christened "Union Ironworks" became a highly profitable investment for Carnegie. But at this moment it was one of a host of his personal investments. More deals remained to be done and his grand vision for steel was still a decade away.

With the exception of his oil holdings, all of Carnegie's investments leveraged off his position at the Pennsylvania and his relationships with Scott and Edgar Thompson. Having been a stellar telegraph operator, and with the telegraph industry growing rapidly along with the railroads, he was presented with an enticing investment opportunity. The strategy was simple. Start a telegraph company with business guaranteed by the railroads. Take market share from the industry giant Western Union and then sell to Western Union as it consolidated the industry. In 1867 Carnegie launched the Keystone Telegraph Company. But before Western Union moved in, a midsized company, Pacific & Atlantic (P&A), grabbed the prey—a highly profitable transaction for Carnegie and his ever-present partners Scott and

Thompson. Ultimately P&A was bought by Western Union in 1873 at another sizable markup for Carnegie, but this was not enough for the deal-maker. Before the merger was announced he engaged in insider trading by buying P&A stock in advance of the sale. It wasn't illegal but it was clearly unethical.

In 1862 Carnegie with Scott and Thompson organized a bridge building company, Piper and Schiffler; it was later renamed the Keystone Bridge Company. In 1868 Keystone won the contract to build a bridge across the Mississippi at Keokuk, Iowa. In this banner project Carnegie's phenomenal energy and financial acumen may be seen at all levels. Keystone won the contract to build the superstructure for the Keokuk and Hamilton Bridge Company. Carnegie oversaw the project and received significant ownership in the company, later becoming its president. Keystone, of course, subcontracted most of its work to Carnegie's Union mills. He then organized the Iowa Contracting Company to build the railroad and naturally the rail order was awarded to Carnegie's Union mills. From start to finish Carnegie extracted a steady stream of profits from all participants in this venture.

With the Keokuk triumph under his belt, Carnegie pursued an even grander project, again across the Mississippi but this time in St. Louis; it was almost his financial undoing. The St. Louis bridge vaulted 1500 feet across the Mississippi with a main span of 515 feet. It was, in the words of the great architect Louis Sullivan, "spectacular and architectonic." To support the central span two underwater caissons were sunk in the riverbed. This was the same technology used a decade later by John A. Roebling and his son, on the more famous Brooklyn Bridge.

Conjoined in this high-risk project with state-of-the-art engineering was state-of-the-art financing. The St. Louis Bridge Company, with Andrew Carnegie as the principal

owner, was the general contractor, with Keystone and Union supplying the bridge and steel. When Carnegie learned the St. Louis Bridge Company was going to sell bonds to finance the project he quickly seized a new opportunity. He had been successful selling bridges, telegraph lines, and sleeping cars, all to the railroads. Why not sell their bonds? His first stop was Junius Morgan, a rising American banker in London and the father of J. Pierpont Morgan in New York. The little Scotsman with the sparkling eyes and fast patter soon sold him a million dollars' worth of bonds. With Morgan under his belt his already substantial reputation was given a big boost. But then he overreached again. If you could sell pies, why not cakes and cookies? He sold bonds for other projects where he and his partners had equity investments. Unfortunately he sold bonds for the construction of a railroad from Davenport, Iowa to St. Paul, Minnesota. In 1873 the project went bad, the bonds went south, and this signal failure involved Carnegie in litigation for the next dozen years. Pierpont Morgan took notice.

The St. Louis bridge was an engineering and technological marvel but a financial failure. The chief engineer, James B. Eads, brilliant but irascible, was constantly at loggerheads with Andrew Kloman of Keystone. Eads prevailed, Kloman walked out, and it took all of Carnegie's persuasive powers to keep the project moving forward. The project was behind schedule, over cost, and out of money. Carnegie was forced to turn to Pierpont Morgan to advance interim financing. To put it mildly this was not a repeat of his father/son relationship with Junius. With Pierpont Morgan (two years younger than Carnegie), it was more like sibling rivalry. J. P. Morgan did not become the premier financier in America without being a superb judge of character. With Carnegie he was spot on. He could not deny Carnegie's talents and accomplishments, but he failed Morgan's test of character. Carnegie was a fast talker and a sharp dealer—in short, a young man

on the make. Morgan set harsh terms. If the bridge was not completed by December 18, 1873, he would foreclose with disastrous consequences for Carnegie, cascading several levels into his supply chain. He would have done it in a heartbeat, perhaps with some degree of satisfaction. On the final day, December 18, the span was completed and Carnegie was saved. More than the sale of Carnegie's steel interests to Morgan in 1901, the St. Louis bridge project was the pivotal event in Carnegie's career. His business philosophy and operating methods were irrevocably changed by his near-death experience with the St. Louis bridge.

Master of Steel

A confluence of several factors set Carnegie on his course to become the king of steel. First, iron was giving way to steel. Iron was strong, but, because of its high carbon content as a residue of the ore smelting process, it was brittle and prone to failure under sharp stress. Once the carbon content was minimized, the resulting steel retained its strength but became malleable. The first large-scale device to transform iron into steel was patented by an Englishman, Henry Bessemer, in 1855. By means of the Bessemer converter, cold air was injected into the molten iron, reducing the carbon content, thus "converting" iron to steel. During his bond-selling trips to Europe, Carnegie met Bessemer and saw the towering, flaming converters in action. The sight captured his imagination. Second, iron rails were giving way to steel rails. The latter cost twice as much but gave eight times the life. Railroads at that time were "the" big market for steel. And nobody could sell rails like Carnegie.

The Oxford essayist and philosopher Isaiah Berlin once observed that "the fox knows many things, but the hedgehog knows one big thing." Rockefeller (oil) and Ford (automobiles) were hedgehogs; Morgan and Mellon were foxes.

Carnegie was both: until 1872 a fox and thereafter a hedge-hog (steel).

Third, Carnegie had an epiphany of sorts after the near-death experience at St. Louis. He determined to concentrate his talents and efforts in one field: steel. As if he had gotten it all wrong for the first thirty-seven years of his life, in 1872 he proclaimed: "Put all good eggs in one basket and watch the basket." He further amplified: "I believe that the true road to preeminent success in any line is to make yourself master in that line. I have no faith in the policy of scattering one's resources." Although skillfully scatter them he did until he cast his lot with steel.

In 1872 he put together a steel plant syndicate named Carnegie, McCandless & Co. Other partners included Henry Phipps and his brother Tom. The company was capitalized at $700,000 at a time when the average steel plant company was capitalized at $170,000. This expenditure signaled Carnegie's ambition not just to enter the industry but to be its leader, all from a startup plant. He hired the preeminent designer of steel plants, Alexander Holley. But his masterstroke was to hire Captain Bill Jones, who had been passed over for the superintendent job at the Cambria Iron Works in nearby Johnstown. Jones had it all. He was mechanically talented and highly innovative with several inventions to his name. He was a brilliant manager and leader who commanded the unswerving affection of his workforce.

All doubts about Carnegie's ambition were dispelled when the company was invited to the Bessemer Association meeting to discuss a pooling arrangement that allocated market shares to the participating companies. Cambria was given the largest share at 19 percent and Carnegie, as a new company, was generously allocated 9 percent. Carnegie (by his own telling) jumped to his feet and demanded an equivalent 19 percent share, otherwise threatening to use his new

low-cost plant to undercut the others. He knew their costs, and he was confident that he could make good on his threat. He was given his 19 percent. Carnegie's formula for industry dominance was relatively simple: "Cut cost, scoop the market, and run the mill full." He set himself aside from his more established competitors by pushing the limits of his furnaces through more up time and higher temperatures in an operation known as "hard driving." Bill Jones was a great practitioner of "hard driving." Carnegie, much to the consternation of his investors, eagerly ploughed an excessive 80 percent of earnings into expanded capacity and the most technologically advanced equipment.

With Jones as superintendent and William P. Schinn as general manager of the Edgar Thompson Works (E.T.), the Carnegie Steel Company soon moved to a position of leadership because it was a low-cost producer. Carnegie, as the undisputed boss and salesman in chief, managed from afar. He peppered Schinn and Jones with a consistent stream of missives to cut costs and gain market share. Profits were at worst adequate and occasionally quite good, but they were willingly sacrificed on the altar of market share. This was the clear road as Carnegie saw it to industry dominance and vast profits. It was a philosophy the Japanese were to employ with some considerable success a hundred years later.

Frick

To reduce his cost Carnegie reduced wages whenever possible. He also needed low-cost raw material, in particular coke used to smelt iron. The Carnegie Steel Company had only marginal success with its own coke operation. In 1881 this brought him face to face with Henry Clay Frick (fourteen years Carnegie's junior), the "king of coke." This was a meeting of the odd couple: the dour and taciturn Frick and the effervescent Carnegie—a listener and a talker. Bill

Jones summed it up well: " I don't particularly like Frick but you always know where you stand. . . . With Carnegie it's a different matter. He is a sidestepper"—one of the very best. Frick was financially stretched and needed capital; Carnegie needed coke. The initial 1882 investment gave the Carnegie Steel Company 11 percent of H. C. Frick, with Frick as the sole coke supplier to the steel company. Coke costs were dramatically reduced and Carnegie was so fond of the arrangement that, unbeknownst to Frick, he and his partners quietly bought shares from Frick's partners and in three years the Carnegie group had a controlling interest in H. C. Frick. Thus a contentious tone was set early on to the Carnegie/ Frick relationship, one that would yield a bitter harvest in the years to come.

Numerous changes followed. Tom Carnegie died from alcoholism in October of 1886 at age forty-three. Since the forced departure of W. P. Schinn, Tom had served as the Carnegie chairman. Loyal to a fault he skillfully muffled his brother's abrasive thrusts, while generally accomplishing his objectives. In its closeness the Tom and Andy Carnegie relationship was not dissimilar to that of two other rising Pittsburghers, R. B and A. W. Mellon.

In 1899 tragedy struck again as Bill Jones was killed in a converter accident at the Edgar Thompson works. For Carnegie he was the last indispensable man. Tom Scott and Captain Bill Jones were critical to Carnegie's success. The former plucked him from obscurity and the latter forged the weapon (E.T.) that made him the master of steel. Carnegie ended up shortchanging both men. When Tom Scott needed a loan guarantee for his struggling Texas and Pacific Railroad in 1874, Carnegie turned him down. After Jones's death, Carnegie's agents convinced his widow to sign over to the Carnegie Steel Company the fifty-plus patents held by her deceased husband for the paltry sum of $35,000. Carnegie

later admitted that the "Jones" mixer alone saved the company $200,000 a year over the next decade.

In the pivotal year of 1889 Carnegie made two fateful changes, which set the course of Carnegie Steel for the next decade. Henry C. Frick was named president of Carnegie Steel, with an ownership that gradually increased until it equaled that of Carnegie's long-time partner Henry Phipps. In 1881, Bill Jones had hired and mentored an energetic seventeen-year-old, Charlie Schwab, "Smilin' Charlie" as he was called. A good complement to the "unsmiling" Frick, Schwab succeeded Jones at Edgar Thompson. He became a confidant of Carnegie and eventually succeeded Frick as president.

Carnegie's success inspired a number of imitators. In 1881 Carnegie's first steel partner, Andrew Kloman, organized a group to build a competitive mill in Homestead. Thinly capitalized, fighting a sagging steel market, and beset by labor problems, the mill was in trouble from the start. Carnegie bought out the group in 1883 and revived the operations, but labor problems would come back to haunt him.

Homestead

When Carnegie bought the Homestead mill he bought along with it the Amalgamated Association of Iron and Steel Workers. Despite the most advanced equipment and Carnegie Steel's traditionally strong management, the Amalgamated, with only 800 of 3800 Homestead employees, stood in the way of making Homestead another E.T. A price war had broken out with the company's arch-competitor, Illinois Steel. Wages had to be reduced. The more Frick and Carnegie discussed the situation only one satisfactory solution presented itself: the Amalgamated had to go. They had locked it out successfully at E.T. in 1888, and they felt they could do no less at Homestead. Carnegie left for Scotland one week before the contract expired on June 30, 1892.

The facts of the brief but bloody Homestead strike are clear. On July 1, 1892 the Amalgamated, along with most of the nonunion Homestead workers, occupied the plant. The company had advertised for replacement workers in several cities, but before the strikebreakers could arrive the firm had to regain possession of the plant. Toward this end Frick brought in some three hundred Pinkerton "guards" from Philadelphia and barged them, along with arms and ammunition, up the Monongahela to Homestead. Unfortunately and tragically there was a fatal flaw in the plan. The Pinkerton men had no direct access to the plant and had to traverse a no-man's land occupied by a roiling mob of strikers and sympathizers. The Pinkertons were repulsed with an estimated four dead, along with six strikers. This was live "industrial warfare" with gunfire, dynamite, incendiaries, and even a small cannon. There were longer and bloodier strikes in American labor history, but none captured the imagination of the American public as did Homestead.

It was over quickly upon the arrival of the entire Pennsylvania National Guard, 8500 strong, under the command of General George R. Snowden. The workers vacated the plant, and, by the end of July, five hundred strikers had recrossed the picket line, bolstered by replacement workers.

Attempting to make the best of a bad situation, Carnegie tried to stage manage public opinion from his retreat in Scotland. The original script had him playing the "good cop" to Frick's "bad cop." Frick, well cast as the bad guy, had been antilabor in the violence-ridden coal fields and had maintained that posture as president of Carnegie Steel. He made no bones about it. A stunning denouement to the strike and to the reputational balance between Frick and Carnegie occurred on July 23. An anarchist, Alexander Berkman, burst into Frick's office, shot him twice and then knifed him. Frick refused anesthetics so as to guide the surgeon in removing

the bullets from his neck and back. He then remained some time at his desk. Frick's courage did not go unnoticed. While Berkman didn't kill Frick, he did put a bullet through the Homestead strike.

Carnegie was now deep into damage control. His first line of defense was that had he been there it wouldn't have happened. Frick was "young and rash." Of a long line of Carnegie fabrications, this one stands out: "While in Scotland I received the following cable from the leaders of the union of our workmen: 'Kind master tell us what you want us to do and we shall do it for you.'" Not surprisingly the "kind master" could not produce the cable; it never existed. Carnegie's actions before and after the strike compounded matters. Here is a brief sample of his labor pronouncements: "I am a strong believer in the advantages of trade unions. . . . There is an unwritten law among the best workmen: 'thou shall not take another member's job.'" And to British Prime Minister William Gladstone: "The works was not worth one drop of human blood. I wish they had sunk." And finally on wages: "We do pay the highest wages in the world. . . . $2.90 per day." The actual figure was less than half.

The public began to see through these deceptions. The St. Louis Post Dispatch took Carnegie to task: "Ten thousand Carnegie public libraries will not compensate the country for the evils of the Homestead lockout. Say what you will of Frick he is a brave man. Say what you will of Carnegie he is a coward." These harsh words and the judgment of history fell upon Carnegie not because of his labor practices: low wages, long working hours, and the absence of union representation. Carnegie Steel's labor practices were generally in line with those of his competitors and were common throughout the industrial landscape of his time. Widespread industrial unionization would have to wait another forty-five years until John L. Lewis established the Congress of Industrial

Organizations (CIO) in the mid-1930s. What brought well-deserved opprobrium down upon Carnegie was his espousal from a world stage of a progressive and enlightened labor policy while acting in a completely antithetical manner. He piled lie upon lie in a vain attempt to salvage his reputation; it simply made matters worse.

Cashing Out

Relations between Frick and Carnegie, strained by Homestead, steadily deteriorated thereafter. As always, operating from afar, Carnegie constantly prodded Frick, often in the wrong direction. He resisted the adoption of open-hearth steel making (the coming technology replacing the Bessemer converter), and he vetoed the acquisition of prized Mesabi ore fields only to see them pass into the hands of John D. Rockefeller. Seeking a solution to an untenable situation, Frick and Henry Phipps proposed to Carnegie the sale of the entire company. Surprisingly and reluctantly Carnegie agreed, at a price of $250 million. Unfortunately Morgan and Rockefeller declined to bid, leaving only a weak syndicate headed by the Moore brothers. The deal fell through and things spiraled downhill rapidly. Carnegie demanded artificially low coke prices from the Frick Coke Company (which Carnegie Steel controlled), and Frick rightly contended this was unfair to the Frick Company's minority shareholders.

Carnegie's response to the coke dispute was to force Frick out at a bargain basement price. His weapon of choice was the 1881 "Ironclad Agreement." Carnegie, in a rare visit to Pittsburgh in January 1890, presented his ultimatum to the seething Frick. Under the Ironclad Agreement Frick was to receive $1.5 million for his common stock—a small fraction of its true value. Frick exploded: "For years I have been convinced that there is not an honest bone in your body. Now I know you are a goddamn thief." And a rumor had it he

chased Carnegie down the hall. Carnegie, always quick on his feet in more ways than one, beat Frick to the security of his office. Frick took Carnegie to court. Carnegie lost and Frick received an ample $31 million—a nice step up.

During the five years prior to 1900 a massive wave of consolidation swept the steel industry. By 1900 the major players were Carnegie Steel (the largest and strongest), Federal Steel (backed by Morgan) and the Moore brothers' National Steel. Carnegie Steel's principal output was in so-called "heavy products": rails, beams, and plates. It also sold billets and slabs to the nonintegrated producers of "light products," such as tubing, wire, and tinplate. Carnegie's competitors had grown through buying up many of the independent producers of light products. Once these firms had sufficient throughput they began to integrate backward into iron and steel production. Carnegie Steel began to lose significant semifinished business that it had once sold to the recently acquired nonintegrated light product producers. Carnegie had only one recourse. He began to integrate forward into light products, providing an output for his low-cost steel operation. Elbert Gary, the chairman of the United States Steel Corporation, spoke to the severity of Carnegie's threat: "The Carnegie Company would have driven entirely out of business every steel company in the United States."

On November 12 the Carnegie Steel board approved the construction of the world's largest plant for the production of tubular products at Conneaut, Ohio. It was Morgan's worst nightmare. In steel as in other large industries Morgan's vision of the future called for large combines, stable markets, and steady profits. Carnegie, in Morgan's view, was reigning as the "prince of chaos" and posed a distinct threat to the industrial system that Morgan was painstakingly creating.

Charlie Schwab, now thirty-nine, was the chairman of Carnegie Steel. His position was far stronger than Frick's and

he knew how to handle Carnegie. It took a lot of flattery and a little deception; Schwab had all of this in addition to being a world-class manager. Morgan called him into a meeting to sound out his views on the future of the steel industry. Not surprisingly they were right in line with Morgan's. Morgan said he was inclined to buy. Would Carnegie sell? Schwab didn't know and had not told Carnegie about his meeting with Morgan. He said he would find out. Upon the advice of Louise Carnegie, Schwab posed the question to Carnegie after a round of golf. Carnegie reflected and said he would give Schwab an answer the next day. The next morning he handed Schwab a single sheet of paper. Price $400 million for the company and $80 million for the estimated 1900 and 1901 profits, bringing the total to $480 million. The estimated profits were inflated by some $30 million. Morgan didn't care; better to be cheated by Carnegie than to have him destroy the industry. Carnegie's share was $225 million (the equivalent of $4.5 billion in today's dollars). It was at that time the largest liquid fortune in the world.

Redemption

Carnegie was to live another eighteen years. The restless energy he put into business now went with equal force into charitable good works. He once said that the man who dies rich dies disgraced. Carnegie established a pattern of charitable giving long before the sale of Carnegie Steel. In 1892 he gave $2 million to build Carnegie Hall in New York. In 1895 he established the Carnegie Library of Pittsburgh with a $1 million gift. As the library later expanded into the Carnegie Museums, Carnegie's total largesse ran to $25 million. He established over three thousand libraries around the United States and throughout the world—at a cost of $60 million. He gave away nearly eight thousand church organs at a cost of over $6 million. This was a strange gift for the agnostic Carnegie.

His rationale: "It lessened the pain of the sermons." In 1902 he donated $30 million to establish the Carnegie Institution of Washington as a think tank for advanced research in the sciences. Ten million dollars went to establish the Carnegie Trust for the universities of Scotland. A total of $7.5 million, in several tranches, seeded the Carnegie Technology School, later the Carnegie Institute of Technology and finally Carnegie Mellon University. He provided $15 million to create the Carnegie Foundation for the Advancement of Teaching. Among the institutions it has spawned are the Teachers and Insurance Annuity Association, now the giant pension fund TIAA-CREF, and the Educational Testing Service. He gave $5 million for the Carnegie Hero Fund in 1904. In 1911, in order to lift the burden imposed upon him by devising so many specific gifts, he endowed the Carnegie Corporation of New York with $125 million for "the advancement and diffusion of knowledge." Carnegie provided $1.5 million for the construction of the International Peace Palace, the establishment of the permanent Court of Arbitration in the Hague. In 1910 he contributed $10 million, establishing the Carnegie Endowment for International Peace.

Not all of his charitable endeavors came to a successful conclusion. Carnegie was a fervent antiimperialist. Upon learning that the United States would govern the Philippines as a dependency and compensate Spain in the amount of $20 million, he proposed a solution. He offered President William McKinley $20 million to buy the Philippines and then set them free; he never thought small.

It is to the credit of most of the creators of America's fortunes that they have left a significant portion of their wealth to charity, but nobody did it with the energy and creative capacity of Andrew Carnegie. Like an Olympic skier, carving graceful turns, Carnegie closely monitored and carefully crafted his philanthropic endeavors. In a summing up

of Andrew Carnegie's life, it is obvious upon which side the balance of judgment must rest. Carnegie was unique. He had the intellectual capacity of a Bill Gates, the vision of a Sam Walton, the gambler's nerve of a Kirk Kerkorian, the promotional ability of a P. T. Barnum, and the philosophical instincts of . . . an Andrew Carnegie.

3

H. J. HEINZ: CONSUMER APOSTLE

IN THE SECOND HALF OF THE NINETEENTH CENTURY, AS Pittsburgh emerged as one of America's great cities, it did so on the back of heavy industry—steel predominantly, but also glass, oil, and all manner of heavy machinery. Indeed four of the five men the novelist Edith Wharton dubbed the "Lords of Pittsburgh" built their fortunes on heavy industry—Carnegie, Frick, Mellon, and Westinghouse. H. J. Heinz was the odd man out. He built one of the nation's first and greatest branded goods companies. And if you were to be marooned on a desert island with one of the five, Heinz would have been your best bet.

Beginnings
Henry John Heinz was born in 1844, the first of nine children, in the Birmingham section of Pittsburgh on the South Side. He was nicknamed Harry. His mother came from Hesse-Darmstadt, and his father from Bavaria; a scant fifty miles

H. J. Heinz. Library and Archives Division, Sen. John Heinz History Center

separated their villages. When Harry was five they moved to Sharpsburg, and the elder Heinz started a brick making and contracting business.

The Heinz family were staunch Lutherans. Anna Heinz enforced rigid church attendance upon her progeny at an

early age. Harry and his young siblings were the subject of Anna Heinz's endless entreaties on the moral precepts of life. Among her favorites were: "Always remember to place yourself in the other fellow's shoes." And: "Do all the good you can; do not live for yourself." As we shall see, Anna Heinz's moral preachments struck fertile ground in the impressionable young mind of Harry Heinz.

Upon reaching age eight, after school at the Lutheran pastorship, Heinz was put to work in the family's garden and in his father's brick kiln. He immediately began to peddle excess produce to the Heinz's neighbors. By the age of ten he was allocated his own three-quarter acre plot. Two years later he had quadrupled his acreage and drove his goods to an expanding market of local merchants with a horse and cart. At age fourteen he was confirmed in the Lutheran Church (the equivalent of graduation) and briefly attended a local seminary. Despite his solid grounding in religion both at home and at school, the tug of commerce drew him to a business career.

At age fifteen he had not one job but two. He served as his father's assistant at the brickyard and soon as his bookkeeper. More central to our story here, he continued his produce business, bringing into it his two brothers, John and Peter, and two sisters. By 1861 the business grossed $2,400 or $48,000 in today's money.

All this did not quite contain Heinz's energy and in 1865 he bought a half interest in his father's brick business. Three years later he entered into a partnership with L. C. Noble, four years his junior and the son of a prominent Sharpsburg family, to manufacture brick in Beaver Falls, Pennsylvania. Heinz's first move out of the fresh produce business was bottled horseradish. It set his course for the remainder of his illustrious career. Most bottled goods then were served up in green or brown bottles, the natural color of glass. Other producers sometimes cheated their customers by hiding inferior ingredients such as

leaves or wood chips in their opaque bottles. Young Heinz used clear glass bottles to put on display and thus promote the highest quality horseradish you could buy. Calling on the customer, Heinz held the bottle up to the light: "See the quality in the whiteness of the root. Unscrew the cap. Taste the quality." With the advantage of hindsight today we can see through that clear glass the future of a global food products company.

In the floodtide of post–Civil War prosperity Heinz was tapping into the desire of the American housewife to pay a modest premium to be relieved of some of her onerous household chores. Quality ingredients were a must, but in philosophical terms they were a necessary but not a sufficient condition. The consumer had to be convinced that the product was not only good, but better than any competing offering. The product had to be promoted constantly. Branding and advertising would come later but the idea was already there.

The business grew rapidly. Over a two-year period they expanded the product line to include celery sauce, pickled cucumbers, sauerkraut, and vinegar. By 1875 their annual capacity was 3,000 barrels of sauerkraut, 15,000 of pickles, and 50,000 of vinegar. To feed this expanding maw they contracted to take the produce from 800 acres in Illinois. However, the failure of Jay Cooke & Company in 1873 precipitated a financial crisis that caught many businesses in its undertow. It looked for a while like the newly renamed Heinz & Noble might skate through on thin ice. It was not to be.

Heinz's promotional abilities and entrepreneurial talents drove the company's success, but also sowed the seeds of its failure. He tried to do too much too fast. Heinz, superintending the company's finances, juggled money from one account to another all to no avail. During Christmas week 1875, Heinz & Noble filed for bankruptcy. Assets were $110,000 and liabilities $160,000. The bankruptcy not only ruined Heinz; it engulfed his parents as well. Their house and furniture were

levied against and advertised for sheriff's sale. Twice he was arrested and released on bail. He was tried for fraud in January of 1876 and mercifully received an acquittal. Heinz had no money for food. He approached three local grocers with whom he had longstanding relationships; all three turned him down. His diary for Christmas Day 1875 gives witness to his anguish. "I feel as though people were all putting us down because we are bankrupt. . . . A man is nowhere without money. . . . It is hard to lose trade, money, friends and reputation and even parents in trouble. . . . I am more blamed because I did the financing."

Two factors favored Heinz's recovery from the terrible ordeal: his ability and ambition plus his youth (thirty-two). He was badly bent but not broken. He again returned to family. His brother John, his cousin Frederic, and his wife jointly raised $3,000. Sarah Heinz held 50 percent of the stock in the newly named F. & J. Heinz Company, launched February 14, 1876. Heinz was paid $125 to run the company. As he called on the trade he carried with him a small notepad marked M. O. It stood for "Moral Obligations" and listed every one of his Heinz & Noble creditors and the amount of his obligation.

The Road Back

Most industrialists aren't diarists. Heinz was the exception. Observations on his recovery from bankruptcy and his building of a major industrial enterprise are recorded in eighteen slender volumes covering the years 1875 to 1894. He was not writing the history of the H. J. Heinz Company; rather, through his quotidian musings on life, family, business, and religion, the reader gleans much insight into the way driving ambition and a deep sense of humanity are so finely balanced in this remarkable man.

> May 17, 1878: George McNally was caught in the belts of the mustard mill at 6 P.M. and all his clothes were ripped

from his back, and yet not much hurt. God be praised for his mercy.

May 25: Bought a blue business suit today, $17, trying to save.

July 1: Had a chat with Mr. Craig (Grocer), a creditor of H. N. & Co. Told him . . . that my moral obligation to him was 100 cents on the dollar.

November 10: I enjoyed this day very much. Sunday School at 9:15. Met my class. All well. Then to Christ Church to hear Dr. Morgan and to Mission Sunday School at 2 P.M. To class at 6:15. Then to hear Reverend E. M. Wood at 7:30 P.M. at Christ M. E. Church. So on the whole, my day was all taken up except about two hours which I enjoyed with my family.

In July of 1877 all hell broke loose in Pittsburgh. The Pennsylvania Railroad cut wages by 10 percent. The men struck and violence ensued. National Guard units were sent in from Philadelphia. Twenty-nine strikers and guardsmen were killed, and property damage was in the millions. It was the worst labor unrest in Pittsburgh until the Homestead strike. These events left a searing and enduring impression on the mind of Henry Heinz. It would culminate in the Heinz factory system, which eliminated the need for violence through enlightened labor management practices. In 1877 it was little more than a dream. In 1900 it was reality.

The rapid growth of the company and subsequent recovery of Henry Heinz's finances were set against a favorable backdrop of changing American eating habits. Prior to 1870 what you ate was largely what you grew or what your neighbors grew. Fresh fruits and vegetables were available only during the growing season. In winter, salads were confined to cucumbers and pickles. A sea change in the form of transportation (rail) refrigeration and vacuum-sealed cans and jars was gathering momentum. The homemakers' tasks were

onerous, extending far beyond "cooking." She in effect operated a small food preparation factory inside her home. She ground coffee beans, stuffed sausage, churned butter, and pressed cheese.

Heinz was among a small group of visionaries in the food processing business who capitalized on these trends. Heinz was far more than a canner of fruits and vegetables. He was a processor of "reciped products," ready to eat right from the can or jar. "Heinz 57 varieties" and soon hundreds more freed the housewife from some of her mind-numbing domestic duties. He removed a part of her little cottage factory and placed it in an industrial setting.

The key to all this was the preservation of food in sealed glass containers. By heating the sealed container to 240 degrees, microorganisms and enzymes were sterilized and destroyed. Among the reasons Heinz succeeded spectacularly where most others failed or languished was his extended definition of that crucial word "quality." Heinz moved the concept of quality upstream from the factory to the field. He bred improved varieties of seeds and contracted with growers to produce the highest quality raw ingredients specifically for his products. Quality was emphasized and monitored throughout the entire process.

By 1879 Heinz had reached his goal of solvency one year ahead of schedule. The first half of the 1880s saw smooth sailing for the company. Although it was still a small business the Heinz diaries of these years are revealing. 1879: "It takes one dress suit every two years to do me. Then I wear it for every day." On a church social: "If I go I treat others, or I can't go. . . . I never could enjoy myself unless I could make others comfortable." Heinz loved the horses that pulled his sales wagon. 1880: "I saw a span of spotted mares, well matched, and inside of a half hour had tried and bought them. They will make a lovely span to advertise." Drinking was an ongoing problem.

1882: "I had all the wagon salesmen together in my room . . . a talk on temperance."

Early in 1884 Heinz bought a foundry building for use as a vinegar factory. It was destined to be the core of the large North Side complex he began in 1890. It continues in use today. Momentum was building; results for 1884 showed sales of $381,000, or $7.62 million in today's dollars, and profits of $43,860 ($877,200). At long last, on February 3, 1885, Heinz's application for release from bankruptcy was upheld: "Thank God I am a free man."

In 1869 Heinz had married Sallie (Sarah) Sloan Young, who had emigrated from Northern Ireland. Irene was born in 1871, Clarence in 1873, and Howard Covode Heinz in 1877. With the birth of his son Clifford in 1884 his family was completed. In 1883 one important addition to the close-knit Heinz family occurred when Sebastian Mueller, who had just been named general manager of manufacturing, married Henry Heinz's sister Elizabeth. This was very much family as Elizabeth and Mueller were first cousins. The impeccably attired Mueller played a critical role in the Heinz enterprise for the next fifty years. Sebastian and Elizabeth Mueller tragically lost all three of their children early in life. They bequeathed their considerable fortune to Eden Hall Farm, a 375-acre recreation facility for H. J. Heinz girls and alumnae. Eden Hall exists today as a $200 million foundation doing good works in the city of Pittsburgh.

By 1887 the business was scaling rapidly. Pickle cucumbers were being harvested at the rate of 22,000 bushels a week from 12,000 acres in northern Indiana. Henry Heinz began to consolidate his ownership in the company. In 1888 he bought half his cousin Frederic's share and soon after all of his brother John's 17 percent share for $57,000. At the suggestion of his mother Anna he changed the name of the company to the H. J. Heinz Company.

Burgeoning sales dictated an expansion and consolidation of capacity in Pittsburgh. The North Side location of the vinegar factory was chosen, and ample land provided for a succession of buildings. They were all "Pittsburgh Romanesque" structures of glazed pressed brick. In Heinz's words: "All hard brick—no soft at all. The best of everything. Oak posts throughout." He equipped these buildings with the most technologically advanced equipment available, but more importantly he provided every convenience and facility imaginable to humanize the workplace—restaurants, dressing rooms, an emergency hospital, indoor swimming pool, roof garden, and practical courses of instruction. It was an extraordinary achievement for its day.

Advertising

Heinz proudly displayed his array of products at the 1893 Columbian Exposition in Chicago—the White City electrified by Pittsburgh's own George Westinghouse. The McKim, Mead & White–designed agricultural building housing the Heinz exhibit covered nineteen acres. Unfortunately for H. J. Heinz and its U.S. competitors they were located one floor up from the main floor, given over to foreign exhibitors and state agricultural exhibits. Heinz had more space than any other exhibitor. It was done in antique oak and attended by a bevy of attractive young hostesses. But traffic was sparse. Sizing up the situation, Heinz responded immediately. He hired an army of young boys who passed out thousands of small, white baggage-claim-size cards promising the bearer upon presentation at the Heinz exhibit a free souvenir.

The second floor soon groaned with a swarm of souvenir seekers converging on the Heinz exhibit. There they saw a wide array of art objects and antiques while feasting on all manner of H. J. Heinz offerings—and the widely promised free souvenir: "a green gutta-percha pickle one and one quarter

inches long, bearing the name *Heinz*." Driven by the sheer novelty of the promotion it was a home run. Fair officials had to summon local police for crowd control. Foreign exhibitors on the first floor cried foul. In contrast, Heinz's neighboring domestic producers were so delighted with the surging traffic that they hosted a dinner in his honor. Heinz's promotional coup d'état, along with those gutta-percha (later plastic) pickles, became an essential part of the Heinz legend. In Heinz's mind the one thing better than advertising your own product was to let others advertise it for you. The *Saturday Evening Post* called the Heinz pickle "one of the most famous giveaways in merchandising history."

Heinz was the first industrialist to promote his products by inviting the public to tour his model plant operation. By the turn of the century over twenty thousand visitors annually were trooping through the Heinz complex. Highlights of the tour included the stables, can factory, time office, and the baked beans building. All tours concluded with a lecture in the company auditorium and, of course, a memento of one's visit—the ubiquitous plastic pickle. I vividly remember my Conneaut Lake grade school visit in 1951 and my little green pickle.

Heinz had an eye for promotion and advertising unequaled by any of his competitors. He loved horses but exploited their drawing power to the full extent. They were all jet black, of a certain size, and ornamented with lustrous brass trimmings. They pulled white wagons with green trimmings. Had the name Heinz not been easily seen from all sides, few would have doubted the provenance of this handsome equipage. Almost every animal selected for the Heinz delivery elite was personally inspected by either H. J. or Sebastian Mueller.

There was nothing very subtle about Heinz's advertising. He advertised early, he advertised late, and he adver-

tised often. From the beginning he employed "point of sale" material in the stores where his goods were sold; calendars, souvenirs, books, and stamped-out pickle cards, you name it he used it. There was hardly a streetcar in America without a Heinz color card and a four-line verse. Large signs were spotted along almost every railroad mainline. Ten prominent hillsides, including a cliff over San Francisco Bay, proudly blossomed with "Heinz 57." The company owned over four hundred freight cars, each proudly emblazoned with the name Heinz.

Electrical outdoor signs were just beginning to be used, and Heinz was a pioneer. He personally designed New York's first large electric sign at 23rd Street and 5th Avenue. It was six stories high and topped by a giant green pickle forty feet long and bearing the name Heinz. Beneath it the viewer read "57 Good Things for the Table exhibited at the Heinz pier."

Heinz personally seized upon the 57 Varieties slogan. While riding a New York elevated train one day, he glanced at the wall and saw an advertisement for "21 styles of shoes." For some unknown reason he seized upon the number 57. As Heinz recounted: "I jumped off the train at the 28th Street station and began the work of laying out my advertising plans. Within a week the sign of the green pickle with the '57 Varieties' was appearing in newspapers, on billboards, signboards, and everywhere else I could find a place to stick it." What cut Heinz out from the herd? These lines say it all. Heinz excluded only one medium in his all-out advertising assault. He refused to advertise in the Sunday papers.

The crown jewel of Heinz's advertising and promotional efforts was the Heinz Ocean Pier at Atlantic City. In 1898 Heinz bought a pier at the foot of Massachusetts Avenue. As reconstructed, it had a land-side building framed by large pickles and a seaside exhibition hall some three hundred feet out into the ocean. Inside the hall were paintings, bronzes,

tapestries, and curios of all kinds. The centerpiece was a
booth with thousands of Heinz products artistically arranged
in revolving pyramids. A lecture was given with slides provid-
ing the visitor a virtual tour of the Heinz Pittsburgh plant.
Everything was free. The lecture concluded by telling the
visitors they were not "obliged to buy" but, *if* you wanted to
purchase goods, they would be sent directly to your home.
The goods flew out of the Heinz warehouses in response to
pier orders. Unique among Atlantic City's several piers the
Heinz Pier was open year-round—but not on Sundays. This
"crystal palace by the sea" had a forty-six-year run from 1898
until 1944.

The Heinz Model Factory

By 1900 the Heinz complex of seventeen buildings on
Pittsburgh's North Side was a small industrial city. It was a
happy city. Its denizens were primarily female. Opportunities
in teaching and nursing required training these young
women neither had nor could acquire. In those days office
clerks and functionaries were mostly men. Hours were
long—7:00 a.m. to 5:40 p.m., six days a week. Wages were
modest but working conditions were very good. The Heinz
girl began each day in a freshly laundered uniform. A weekly
manicure was required, and she had available to her the
services of a doctor and two dentists. She could enjoy her
modest leisure time on a rooftop garden, in the reading
room, swimming, or in the gymnasium. Classes in a variety of
self-improvement activities included dressmaking, drawing,
and even singing. For new immigrants citizenship instruction
was offered. His last contribution to the North Side complex
was a large brick and marble social service center for chil-
dren constructed at the vast sum of $500,000 ($10 million
in today's money). It was named the Sarah Heinz House in
honor of his deceased wife.

The Heinz auditorium provided lectures and concerts of top quality. John Philip Sousa, Victor Herbert, and Walter Damrosch were among the noted conductors. For its day the Heinz factory system was a spectacular achievement, and Heinz's fingerprints were on every part of it. Ever the promoter, Heinz was not bashful about publicizing his model factory. He received international awards in Paris and at Leige, Belgium. At the St. Louis Fair in 1904 he received a grand prize for "placing factory conditions on a higher plane and developing employees into comfortable, happy, ambitious and more intellectual workers." Heinz willingly met the press to answer questions about his signal achievements in employee relations. Asked if he received value for his expenditures, Heinz said: "I have never given that side of the matter any thought." This of course was somewhat ingenuous and, when pressed on the matter, Heinz replied: "Very well then, if you don't like the sentiment that attaches to the plan, I want you to distinctly understand that it is good business as well. It pays." Heinz was no utopian sentimentalist; he had ever in mind the endgame. Not surprisingly there was no labor trouble at Heinz, and unions came only in the sweeping organization drives of the 1930s.

The Pickle King

By 1900 Heinz had built the nation's largest packaged foods company. The firm's market share rankings in leading product categories was impressive by any measure. It held the largest share in pickles, vinegar, sauerkraut, horseradish, and, most importantly, its future flagship product—ketchup. It was second in mustard and fourth in olives. H. J. Heinz employed 2,800, of whom 400 were salesmen. Behind this industrial phalanx stood an army of 20,000 who grew Heinz-contracted crops on 16,000 acres. Aside from a couple of minor acquisitions, Heinz's growth was organic.

The company's high profile, carefully cultivated at every opportunity by Henry Heinz, attracted the interest of money men in New York and London. His answer, given full venting by the press, was not surprising: "I do not care for your money. . . . I love this business. To stop work is death—mentally and physically. This business is run—not for my family . . . but for what we call the Heinz family—the people who make our goods and sell them." Heinz was not ready to sell but was ready to step back a bit. In 1900 he was fifty-six—with today's life span the equivalent of sixty-six. The company was run by an eight-man advisory board, chaired not by Heinz but by Heinz's brother-in-law and right-hand man, the indispensable Sebastian Mueller. The board met daily but Heinz limited his attendance to one appearance a week when he was in town. For a while Heinz even considered limiting the company sales to $15 million annually, $300 million in today's money. Fortunately this idea died stillborn.

While still having ironclad control, after 1905 Heinz gradually morphed into the role of chief salesman and promoter. Heinz knew and valued the Heinz horses, but he was always ready for the next new thing—in this case, the gas-driven delivery truck. In 1904 Heinz moved the original Sharpsburg house—"The House Where We Began"—to the North Side plant. The 16-ton house was rolled to the Allegheny and floated down to the North Side. It was a monumental job and naturally Heinz provided for full press coverage. "The House Where We Began" became an essential part of the Heinz factory tour.

In 1892 Heinz purchased the Hopkins mansion Greenlawn in the Breezewood section of Pittsburgh. His neighbors included George Westinghouse, Henry Clay Frick, R. B. Mellon, and a host of Carnegie partners including Carnegie's mother. Greenlawn occupied a full block on Penn Avenue between Lang and Murtland Avenues. It was more than a

mansion; it was a museum and a conservatory. By 1915 it had some five thousand possessions covering a bewildering variety of objects: miniatures, antique watches, glass, pottery, jewelry, and silver to name a few. He had a full-time curator. He built a full-blown conservatory consisting of ten greenhouses, almost a small private Phipps Conservatory. The museum and the conservatory were closely intertwined with his constant travels.

Heinz lost his wife Sarah in 1894. He never remarried. His two eldest sons, Clarence and Howard, were brought into the business. Clarence, plagued by bad health, was not cut out for a business life and retired from the company in 1914. Howard more than measured up to his father's high expectations and succeeded him as president upon his death in 1919.

From the day he founded the company, H. J. Heinz was uncompromising about the quality of his products. As national branded goods replaced the labels of local wholesalers, quality became even more important. Chemical adulterants were widely used as food preservatives, and all too often they disguised inferior and sometimes harmful ingredients. The hero of the struggle of consumer protection was a Civil War veteran, chemistry professor, and finally chief chemist of the Agricultural Department, Dr. Harvey Washington Wiley. He had no more staunch ally in his long struggle for pure food legislation than Henry Heinz and the H. J. Heinz Company. In 1902 he dispatched the redoubtable Sebastian Mueller and his son Howard to the White House to press the case with the progressive Theodore Roosevelt. Only, in this case, Roosevelt proved to be not so progressive; he was skeptical of maverick businessmen pleading altruistic intentions.

Wiley orchestrated a campaign through the national press and through state food and dairy associations. Pressure built. In 1905 a six-member committee representing organized interests on behalf of a pure food law returned to the White House; Sebastian Mueller was the only representative of a major

company. This time Roosevelt agreed to prepare legislation. It passed the Senate but languished in the House. Then Upton Sinclair published his sensational novel *The Jungle* about conditions in the Chicago packing houses. The Pure Food and Drug Act was passed in 1907. Theodore Roosevelt bowed to national acclaim. Wiley was soon forgotten; Heinz played an indispensable role in the enactment of this landmark legislation.

Heinz turned sixty in 1905. While his word was still law on any matter he might choose, the fortunes of the company were firmly in the hands of Howard and Sebastian Mueller. His wealth and prominence permitted Heinz to focus upon broader social and spiritual issues and to travel to an even greater extent than he had done before.

He was most widely known as the founder and patriarch of the H. J. Heinz Company, but as the result of his world travels he won widespread acclaim as an art patron, a political campaigner, and, most importantly, a religious leader.

Heinz had been active in Sunday School from childhood as a pupil, teacher, superintendent, and director of the county association. In 1906 he succeeded his friend John Wanamaker (the Philadelphia department store king) as the president of the Pennsylvania State Sabbath School Association. He also served on the executive committees of the World and International Sunday School Associations.

During the half century from the Civil War to the First World War religion had a social pervasiveness far different from the sharp political thrust of today's religious right. Religion as a social instrument subtly wrapped its tendrils around the social life of the community. Indeed, to be a member of the community was virtually synonymous with being an active member of a community church. In order to tease out the full dimensions of Heinz's life we must underline his commitment in time and money to this religious community. Heinz understood the Sunday School movement

to be "the world's greatest living force for character building and good citizenship." The most powerful force that drew Heinz into his Sunday School work was his love of children. From early on he had an innate understanding of children. He responded to them and they reciprocated. A Heinz company director once said: "He loved children more than any man I knew. I don't think he ever saw a child without giving it something." The International and World Sunday School Associations were essentially peace movements. They had taken deep root in the near century of peace in the world since the fall of Napoleon in 1815. Unfortunately catastrophe was near at hand.

In March 1913 he undertook a round-the-world trip through the Orient to attend the seventh convention of the World Sunday School Association in Zurich. His oldest son Clarence (thirty-nine) accompanied his father. His youngest son Clifford (twenty-nine) was working with his brother Howard in Pittsburgh. The trip was by no means strictly confined to World Association business. In today's terms Heinz was an inveterate multitasker. Countless boxes of the company's 57 varieties accompanied his entourage, and he was always on the lookout for new agents and distributors of Heinz products throughout the world. Earlier trips to Europe had established Heinz U.K. as a leading force in European markets. On the artistic side he was always on the lookout for new additions to his growing and varied collections.

Heinz was also active in local politics. He was one of the leaders in the fight to merge the city of Allegheny with seven square miles and population of 150,000 with the city of Pittsburgh. As the largest employer in Allegheny and a prominent resident of Pittsburgh he played a pivotal role. The merged municipality in 1906 advanced from twelfth to sixth place in the United States—a high watermark in both its ranking and influence.

Under Howard and Sebastian Mueller the Heinz Company was a well-run and expanding enterprise. Henry Heinz generally thought so but not always. He occasionally interfered—not in matters of major importance but on minor items that happened to seize his attention. Unsatisfied with the company's California sales he urged more local advertising. He wrote to Howard: "I now insist that we act. I urged this before I left home but cannot find a single advertisement in the magazines. Are you asleep? Read this to the advertising department." And then in a repentant mood a few days later: "I am preaching a little this morning because I feel deeply. If I love you I must speak the truth and say the things that will help you." His wisdom in letting go of the business provides a sharp contrast to the monumental yet tyrannical figure of Henry Ford who browbeat and bullied his only son Edsel to an early grave in 1943.

Heinz liked new things. In 1911 when visiting Heinz's operations in northern Indiana he went for an airplane ride with aviation pioneer Glenn Curtis. They covered (appropriately) fifty-seven miles in one hour and fifteen minutes.

Heinz was always slender and dapper. Most people try to lose weight; Heinz tried to gain it during his annual trip to the spa at Bad Kissingen. In notes on his stay Heinz observed: "All puddings and vegetables contain plenty of butter. I manage to eat one-third of a pound of butter per day." His trip was not a complete success. He gained only three and one-half pounds in ten days.

Henry J. Heinz died on May 14, 1919, six months short of his seventy-fifth birthday. He left an estate of $4 million ($80 million in today's dollars). Major bequests were $250,000 to the University of Pittsburgh and $300,000 to various Sunday School associations. He offered Greenlawn's conservatory to the City of Pittsburgh. The city declined the offer and a few years later the entire site was razed and subdivided. The balance of the estate was divided in equal portions

between Irene, Howard, and Clifford—Clarence had been separately provided for.

Among Edith Wharton's "Lords of Pittsburgh," the Heinz fortune was by far the smallest. But through the careful stewardship of Howard, who succeeded his father as president and held the office until his death in 1941, and his younger brother Clifford, the Heinz legacy grew through their bequests to the Heinz endowments comparable in size to the R. K. Mellon Foundation. How did so little relatively turn into so much? H. J. Heinz built a superior company in a good industry. Its fortunes prospered and its stock compounded more rapidly than the heavy industrial holdings of his peers.

Fortune building often takes a terrible toll on the builder, his family, former friends, and weaker competitors. However, no matter how hard one sands the varnish the unvarnished truth about Heinz remains the same—he led a balanced life; he had a human touch. His story is about good products produced by a good man.

4

THE AMAZING CAREER OF GEORGE WESTINGHOUSE

IN PITTSBURGH, THE HOME OF WESTINGHOUSE ELECTRIC and Westinghouse Air Brake, the name Westinghouse is well known, although since the disappearance of Westinghouse Electric as an independent company and a reflagging of Westinghouse Air Brake into Wabtec, name recognition is on the decline. Many Pittsburghers know that George Westinghouse founded both companies but few of us know much beyond that.

My interest in George Westinghouse began one dreary fall day when, at the suggestion of my longtime friend, Ed Clarke, formerly president of the Westinghouse Industry Products Company, we visited the George Westinghouse Museum in Wilmerding, Pennsylvania, about twelve miles from downtown Pittsburgh. The museum is housed inside the former Westinghouse Air Brake offices, a gray stone building with a hint of the medieval, appropriately named "the Castle."

George Westinghouse. Courtesy of the Library of Congress

Nobody has done more to keep the memory of George Westinghouse alive than Ed Reis, the executive director of the museum and a veteran Westinghouse Electric employee. During our visit, Ed recounted a remarkable story about a man, nearly unique in the annals of American economic history. In his sixty-eight years, George Westinghouse had, to his credit, over 361 patented inventions. As well, he founded sixty companies around the world, including two Fortune 500 companies. In the pantheon of American inventors he is surpassed only by Thomas A. Edison. As an industrialist he deserves

admittance into a small circle, including Carnegie, Ford, and Rockefeller. As an inventor/industrialist he stands by himself.

Yet strangely we know little about this man. Rockefeller and Ford had their occasionally tarnished reputations burnished by Ivy Lee and Samuel Crowther respectively, and Carnegie, ever conscious of his public image, did it brilliantly by himself. George Westinghouse never lifted a finger to claim his rightful place in history. He seldom gave interviews and refused but on the rarest of occasions to have his picture taken. To their everlasting credit, Carnegie, Ford, and Rockefeller left behind what are now multibillion dollar foundations. Despite dying a wealthy man, Westinghouse left everything to his heirs; there is no Westinghouse foundation.

As if all this was not enough, Westinghouse left no paper trail: records of interviews, speeches, internal memos, personal letters, hardly anything survives. Consciously or unconsciously he pretty much scuttled any attempt to produce a readable or interesting biography, quite necessary to keep his reputation alive and in the public mind. While the shelves groan with biographies of Carnegie, Ford, and Rockefeller, we only have two biographies of Westinghouse, the last being published in 1922. Neither is exactly a page-turner.

Beginnings

The U.S. economy shot out of the Civil War like a coiled spring. The post–Civil War era gave rise to American big business and the first big business was railroads. As the noted economic historian Alfred E. Chandler tells us in *The Visible Hand*, the railroad industry set the pattern for all the major industrial enterprises to come in its wake. It was the railroad industry that created the demand that fueled the growth of the American steel industry.

Hard upon the heels of the industrial infrastructure provided by railroads and steel, the electrical revolution played

out over the thirty-year period beginning in 1890. Electricity spread industry and commerce into every nook and cranny of America, completing our transition from an agrarian to a manufacturing economy. From Appomattox to Sarajevo, from 1865 to 1914, George Westinghouse was intimately involved with the creation of the world's largest and most technologically advanced economy.

The eighth of ten children, George Westinghouse was born in a small village near Schenectady, New York in 1846. His father, also George Westinghouse, was of Westphalian stock, the name having been Anglicized from Westinghausen. George Westinghouse, Sr. was the proprietor of a small shop manufacturing a variety of machinery for agricultural and industrial applications. The elder Westinghouse was also an inventor of sorts and had seven patents to his name. Ironically, the little shop, proudly bearing the sign "G. Westinghouse & Co." still stood many years later alongside the main gate at General Electric's mammoth Schenectady works.

The young Westinghouse went to work for his father at fifty cents an hour in 1860. Metalworking and machinery were in the very air that he breathed. Like countless thousands on both sides of the Civil War, George Westinghouse ran off to enlist in the Union army at the tender age of fifteen. His father grabbed him back, but, two years later, in 1863, with his father's consent he enlisted in the infantry and soon became an engineer in the Union Navy. He was mustered out of the service at age nineteen. After three months at tiny Union College, his formal education was over and he was back at his father's shop.

He was nineteen when his first patent for a rotary steam engine was issued in 1865. His last patent was issued fifty-three years later in 1918, four years after his death. Married at twenty in 1867, the Westinghouses died, after forty-seven years of marriage, three months apart in 1914. They are buried

side by side in Arlington National Cemetery. Their only child, George Westinghouse III, worked for his father but moved to California in 1916 and then to Canada in 1926.

During the four years between 1869 and 1873, George Westinghouse was issued more than twenty patents on the revolutionary air brake. This was one of the great inventions of the nineteenth century, and it laid the foundation for his fame and fortune. In developing his phalanx of patents on the air brake he learned from his prior mistakes. His first attempts at patented railroad products were a device to rerail derailed cars, called a "car replacer," and a "frog" to switch a train onto new tracks. They were practical successes but commercial failures. Both were adopted by the railroads who sidestepped his modest patent protection, yielding him little return. But he was a fast learner and didn't make the same mistake twice.

By 1873, the young Westinghouses had moved to Pittsburgh. It was a major railroad hub, offering low-cost steel and an ample pool of trained mechanics to work it. For a young man with proven mechanical aptitude, inventive genius, and overwhelming ambition, it was the ideal place to be—the Silicon Valley of its day. His attorneys, Bakewell, Christy and Kerr, artfully wove a web of patent protection around the ample flow of air brake improvements springing from Westinghouse's drawing board. This time the patents held and the railroads paid; they paid big. Westinghouse was on his way to being a leading industrialist in a growing and vibrant city.

Steel Wheels on Steel Rails

Before the advent of the air brake, rail cars were stopped by a brakeman on each car laboriously turning a wheel to apply the brakes. The original Westinghouse air brake patent, #88929, was dated April 13, 1869. In the next seven years, 38 percent of the nation's rolling stock used his product. The number of

feet required to bring the average train to a dead stop from thirty miles per hour was reduced from 1600 feet to 500 feet. Buttressed by a blizzard of 103 inventions from 1869 to 1907, Westinghouse Air Brake held the market in a vise-like grip.

The economic implications of the automatic air brake were staggering. Longer trains running at higher speeds caused rail haulage costs to drop precipitously. With notable improvements over time, the automatic air brake has been used continuously for 119 years—and still counting. His contribution to the railroad industry was no single-act play. To replace railcar coupling springs he invented the friction draft gear. A. J. Cassart, president of the Pennsylvania Railroad, once said that the friction draft gear was equal in importance to the air brake.

Finally, the increase in railroad traffic soon necessitated a system of signals and switches that were interlocked with one another to ensure adequate distance between trains and to give the right of way to one train over another, avoiding collisions. Over a two-year period during 1881 and 1882, Westinghouse patented eighteen inventions in switch and signal control. In 1881 he established the Union Switch and Signal Company which was later merged into Westinghouse Air Brake. Backed by critical patents and a broad vision of where the field was going, Union Switch and Signal came to dominate the business.

By century's end power signaling and interlocking was the third and final act of the product line that George Westinghouse developed for the railroads. Along with the friction draft gear, signal interlocking unleashed the full potential of the air brake. Together they gave us the modern rail system that we know today.

Interlude

In 1883, Westinghouse became interested in natural gas. As usual, he wasted little time. He applied for twenty-eight pat-

ents in 1884 and 1885, with ten more to follow. His gas inventions included the proportional gas meter, automatic cutoff regulator, pressure regulator valve, and long-distance gas transmission through a series of increasing-diameter lines in lieu of lines of uniform dimension; the list goes on.

His most intriguing invention is innocuously termed: well drilling apparatus, Patent #307606, 1884. A summary of the invention reads: "The invention combines rotary cutting apparatus and a fluid-pressure motor actuating it." Sound familiar? With #307606, Westinghouse came within a hair's breadth of beating "Big Howard" Hughes to the invention of the rotary drill bit, the foundation of his son's erratically run empire.

When George Westinghouse went into a new industry such as natural gas, he jumped in with both feet. Much to the doubtless dismay of Mrs. Westinghouse and his neighbors, George punched down a well right in his own backyard at Solitude, his residence in Homewood. As usual, he was successful; gas was struck in a moderate amount at eight hundred feet. This was quite sufficient to serve his own needs and those of a few neighbors; but now caught up in the excitement, Westinghouse pushed on. A few hundred feet later, with a roar, came a flaming blast of gas along with tools and the casing head. For several weeks he brightened his neighborhood with a roaring torch one hundred feet high. He had his own Spindletop.

In order to market his inventions in the natural gas industry, Westinghouse founded the Philadelphia Company in 1882. It produced and distributed natural gas as well as electricity in the Pittsburgh area. For many years it ran the streetcar systems of Pittsburgh and San Francisco.

Unlike many other inventors, Westinghouse never sold a patent. All his patented inventions were brought to life with the sole aim of expanding a business enterprise in which he played a triple role of inventor, executive, and financier. With

Westinghouse it was not so much a matter of money as it was always making things better by solving a succession of technological challenges. To this degree he was an early precursor of the Japanese system of "kaizen," or continuous improvement. As abruptly as he had thrust himself into the natural gas business, he now moved on to a much bigger challenge.

The Main Event

Had the life of George Westinghouse been tragically foreshortened before the age of forty, his reputation as an inventor of the first rank and industrialist of note would have been secure. Fortunately, all this was merely prelude to an extraordinary thirty years to come. In the words of the famous singer Al Jolson: "You ain't heard nothing yet."

To understand the role George Westinghouse was to play in the electrical revolution, which was at hand in 1886, we must turn to Thomas Edison, the Wizard of Menlo Park—America's greatest inventor. Edison's work with electricity brought forth a stunning series of inventions including notable improvements to the telegraph and the telephone, along with the invention of the phonograph, all laying the foundation for his invention of the incandescent light bulb.

Having conceived of a product of great practical utility and universal application, Edison was now driven to build a generating and transmission system to bring light to the millions. For starters he announced he would light up lower Manhattan. In September of 1882, Edison's Pearl Street generating station sprang to life. Edison made good on his claim.

The direct current (DC) generator had one serious drawback. The low voltage incandescent bulb limited the DC service area to five hundred yards. Alternating current (AC) operating at high voltage can be transmitted great distances. The missing piece of the puzzle was a transformer capable of "stepping up and stepping down" AC current. Moving with

his usual dispatch, Westinghouse bought the U.S. patent to the Gaulard Gibbs transformer. The newly founded (1886) Westinghouse Electric Company improved upon the Gaulard Gibbs transformer, turning it into a workable product, which provided the backbone for an AC distribution system. By the end of 1886 Westinghouse Electric had orders for twenty-seven new systems.

Nicholas Tesla was a highly educated Serbian inventor who wrapped his genius in formal attire and old-world eccentricities. He worked for Edison briefly but struck out on his own. At the end of 1887 he filed for seven U.S. patents that were among the most important in the history of the electrical industry. They covered AC, motors supported by a complete system, including generation, transformers, transmission lines, and lighting.

Westinghouse Electric had been patiently putting pieces of this puzzle together, and the company brain trust in Pittsburgh told Westinghouse they could get to the finish line. Instead, Westinghouse, with a Hail Mary pass, went for the main chance. Tesla had it all. He paid Tesla $60 thousand in cash and Westinghouse stock and agreed to pay him $2.50 per horsepower on all AC capacity the company sold. This overgenerous royalty kicker showed that even the ever-optimistic Westinghouse had no idea how big the market would become. It was the best deal he ever made; it was the best deal Tesla ever made.

Westinghouse viewed the lighting contract at the 1893 Chicago World's Fair, also known as the Columbian Exposition, as a blue ribbon prize. The front-running competitor was the newly formed General Electric Company (GE) backed by Edison and the Morgan interests. The contract called for 92,000 lights to illuminate the fair; it was called the "White City." Westinghouse, the underdog, was confident that by providing a complete AC system to power the exposition it would

be worth the price. It was; the blazing lights of the "White City" were seen by millions and read about by tens of millions more.

Unfortunately, weeks before the fair opened, Westinghouse lost a patent case with GE, denying Westinghouse the use of the GE incandescent bulb. With only days to spare, Westinghouse delivered a new "stopper lamp" that, though inferior to the GE lamp, lit the fair as promised. The generating plant that powered the fair was at that time the largest AC central station in existence.

From Chicago it was on to Niagara Falls. Water has long been used as a direct power source and in the closing years of the nineteenth century it began to be used to generate electricity. There was no better opportunity than Niagara Falls. To pursue this enormous project, an East Coast financial syndicate capitalized the Cataract Construction Company in late 1899, with $2,630,000. The proposal called for a mind-numbing one hundred thousand horsepower of generating capacity, exceeding all the central station capacity then installed. By 1891 there were over one thousand Westinghouse AC stations, five times the number of Edison DC stations. The Niagara Falls contract was sure to settle the question of leadership once and for all. After six months of twists and turns, including purloined Westinghouse blueprints that found their way to GE and a futile attempt on the part of the Cataract Company to design its own generators, by October of 1893 Westinghouse had the contract.

There remained however one more piece of the puzzle. Niagara Falls was not a lighting plant like the Columbian Exposition's "White City"; it was a power plant. The bulk of the power generated at Niagara Falls had to go to Buffalo and beyond. The power was stepped up and then stepped down to 440 volts and delivered at first to Buffalo streetcars and then throughout the city. The long distance transmission of AC power was now a proven reality.

The twin triumphs of the Columbian Exposition and Niagara Falls were, in the words of the Duke of Wellington on Waterloo: "A near thing." George Westinghouse was intimately involved at every stage of the game. His technological versatility, his entrepreneurism, his manufacturing capability, and, above all, his force of personality carried the day.

This triumph was all the more remarkable in the face of the dire financial straits he found himself in. The collapse of the British Barings Bank in 1891 tightened the credit markets, which hit home just as Westinghouse Electric was riding a surge of growth with inadequate capital. Financially George Westinghouse simply cut it too thin. Here he stands in sharp contrast to the fiscally prudent Andrew Carnegie, who was always prepared to ride out a downturn and gain ground on his rivals at the same time. Turned down by Pittsburgh bankers in 1891, Westinghouse got the money he needed in New York, but a critical stumbling block was the generous royalties he had agreed to pay Nicholas Tesla. In a dramatic gesture Tesla tore up his contract, thus saving Westinghouse Electric from reorganization and the loss of control by its founder. In the later years of Tesla's life this action condemned him to relative poverty.

After Niagara Falls the Westinghouse Electric Company grew to be a major industrial corporation. By 1907 sales had reached $35 million, equivalent to $700 million today. However, the financial panic of 1907 struck Westinghouse hard. Westinghouse lost control and the East Coast bankers put their own man in to rein in the expansionist bent of the founder. By 1910 Westinghouse was no longer on the board. As he traveled from Homewood to Wilmerding, the sight of the mammoth works at East Pittsburgh was always painful.

Taking His Measure

As an inventor George Westinghouse was second only to Thomas Edison—a close second. For a forty-nine year period

George Westinghouse produced on average one invention every seven weeks—over 361 in all. Westinghouse founded sixty-one companies, a number of them significant, including two Fortune 500 companies. At its peak the Westinghouse Air Brake Company ranked 185th in 1957. Westinghouse Electric Company was the 13th largest industrial corporation in America in 1955, 1959, and 1971. Although he lost control of the electric company in 1907, at his death he left an estate of $50 million, or the equivalent of $1 billion today.

George Westinghouse was also recognized as one of the most progressive industrial employers. He built the town of Wilmerding and provided it with a host of services for his Air Brake employees. He was the first major Pittsburgh industrialist to reduce the workweek from six to five and a half days. There were no Homestead strikes in his legacy.

It is not surprising that, in patent law, frequent mention is made of: "The state of the art." Inventions, while aimed at practical matters, are to a degree art, and, by extension, the inventor is an artist. Inventors, by and large, don't make good businessmen. Henry Ford comes to mind as a stunning exception. As an inventor he falls far short of Westinghouse, but, of course, as an industrialist he was incomparably superior. The remarkable thing about Westinghouse is how well he balanced his extraordinary talents. In this respect he is almost unique in the annals of American economic history.

Despite doing everything possible to leave no footprints and thus diminish his reputation, proper due diligence fast brings us to the conclusion that he was Pittsburgh's preeminent industrial figure. To take a refrain from a popular song of the 1960s, "Wichita Lineman," George Westinghouse is all around us today: "we can hear him singing in the wires."

Note

My great thanks to Ed Clarke who started me on my journey with George Westinghouse; to Ed Reis who critiqued the manuscript; and to Bill Kassling, the CEO of Wabtec, who told me about air brakes.

5

BLOOD PACT: THE STORY OF HENRY CLAY FRICK

AMONG THE GREAT FORTUNES OF PITTSBURGH'S GOLDEN age (1870–1910) that of Henry Clay Frick stands third, bested only by Andrew Carnegie and the Mellons. But the extraordinary aspect of the Frick fortune was not its size. Carnegie, Heinz, Mellon, and Westinghouse were all entrepreneurs. They exercised ultimate control over the fate of their operations. Frick started as an entrepreneur, but his fortune was earned largely as a manager and chief executive officer. He is likely the best CEO this town has ever seen; beyond doubt he was the highest paid.

Henry Clay Frick, named for Henry Clay, former Speaker of the House of Representatives and known as the "Great Compromiser," was born in West Overton, Pennsylvania, north of Connellsville, on December 19, 1849. On his mother's side Frick came of distinguished local lineage. Elizabeth Overholt Frick was one of eight children of Abraham and

Henry Clay Frick. Courtesy of the Library of Congress

Maria Overholt; they were Mennonites. Abraham, in addition to extensive property holdings, owned two distilleries. One was at Overton (he also owned the one-street village), and a large complex on the banks of the Youghiogheny at Broad Ford. Frick's father, John, worked as a hand at the Overholt distillery and later scratched out a near subsistence living as a farmer. The formative influences on young Clay, as he was called, came almost exclusively from the Overholt side. In the young eyes of Clay, Grandpa Overholt was a rich and magnetic figure.

Never pleased with their daughter's marriage to the hapless John Frick, the Overholts lived in relative opulence and did little to help the struggling Frick family. Clay both resented and emulated Abraham Overholt. He told his sister Maria: "Oh I'll be worth $200,000 some day." That day would come sooner than he could possibly realize.

He began his business career in 1863 at the age of fourteen by clerking in his uncle Christian Overholt's store in West Overton. Two years later he moved to Mt. Pleasant, continuing his clerking career for his uncle Martin Overholt. He had sporadic college training at nearby Westmoreland College and Otterbein in Ohio; it was very thin varnish.

During this five-year apprenticeship he began to manifest the traits that were to make him a major industrialist. Abraham Overholt was an immaculate dresser, and, within his limited means, young Clay adopted his mode of dress. He impressed the patrons at his stores with his precise dress and manners, not with a salesman's natural banter. At age nineteen he went to work for his cousin Abraham Tintsman at the Broad Ford distillery—still within the Overholt orbit. He quickly mastered the skills of bookkeeping. The books were kept with neatness and precision; his handwriting was almost artistic. He was fascinated by the cash circulatory system of inflows and outflows. Growing confidence turned to brashness one day when his grandfather Overholt visited: "Grandfather won't you tell me near as you can what my share in your estate would be? If I had it [now] I could make so much more out of it than you are." Clay Frick soon got his answer. Abraham died in 1870 leaving 10% or $40,000 ($800,000 in today's money) to Clay's mother—his direct share: zero.

Beneath the rolling croplands around Connellsville lay the richest vein of metallurgical coal in the United States—the eponymous Connellsville seam. Henry Clay Frick at twenty-one had the business acumen, the family connections, and, most importantly, the vaulting ambition to ride its bounteous harvest to staggering success. He moved quickly.

Coke was gradually replacing charcoal and anthracite coal as the fuel of choice for smelting iron. Coke was produced in the sixty-mile-long Connellsville coal fields by means

of beehive ovens. They were twelve feet in diameter and seven feet high. Coal was fired in an airless chamber for forty-eight hours. Sulfur, phosphorous, and other impurities were burned off leaving a residual of nearly pure carbon. With burgeoning iron making in nearby Pittsburgh, an inexhaustible supply of raw material, and relatively low capital costs, coke making offered an irresistible opportunity.

In 1871 Frick confidently borrowed $75,000 against his mother's share of Abraham Overholt's estate. He went into business with his cousins J. S. R. Overholt and Abraham Tintsman on land adjacent to Tintsman's Broad Ford distillery. Frick was the active partner, and the company soon became known as Frick & Company.

The years from 1871 to 1881 were years of frenetic activity for Frick. Hard upon the launch of the firm, Frick sought a $10,000 loan from a business associate of Abraham Overholt, the formidable Judge Thomas Mellon. Frick was highly leveraged, and the loan was backed more by Frick's character than by hard assets. The young man's dress, demeanor, and intensity quickly won the judge over. With his oven project only half completed, Frick asked for another loan to increase capacity. The loan officer at the bank turned him down, but the judge intervened. He sent his own mining partner, James B. Corey, down to the Connellsville fields for an on-site inspection. Corey was duly impressed and reported back to the judge: "Give him the money. Land's good, ovens well built; manager on job all day, keeps books evenings. Maybe a little bit too enthusiastic about pictures but not enough to hurt; knows his business down to the ground."

Business was good, but in 1873 a financial panic sent the U.S. economy into a tailspin. Frick weathered the storm but it was a close call. His work schedule gives a clue as to his survival. Up at 3:00 a.m. he monitored his own coke ovens and later went surveying a host of distressed properties. By 10:00

a.m. he was in Pittsburgh soliciting coke orders—then back to Connellsville to do the books and catch some sleep. Tintsman, on the way to bankruptcy, sold his shares back to Frick.

Tintsman was also about to shut down the feeder railroad he owned, with potentially disastrous consequences for Frick. Quite imaginatively Frick employed a railroad solution to solve a railroad problem. Quickly he rounded up controlling options at distressed prices and then sold the railroad to the B & O, convincing them that it would be a big money maker when coking activity returned to normal. The deal was done. Frick could get his coke to the market, and for his efforts he asked for and received a $50,000 commission. Hard pressed, his other partners sold their shares in the company back to Frick—paid for with his commission money. By 1875 he was the sole owner of Frick & Company. However, opportunities to buy distressed properties kept coming his way. He continued buying properties but avoided excessive leverage by bringing in two partners. A constant buyer, he often pressed his luck but never to the brink. In 1878 he had a thousand ovens producing nine thousand tons or a hundred carloads of coke a day. Not yet thirty years old, he was a millionaire and had earned the title of the "coke king."

Frick deepened his ties to the Mellon family through his friendship with A. W. Mellon. In 1880, when A. W. was twenty-five (six years younger than Frick) the judge gave him full ownership and control of T. Mellon & Sons. From that day forward his word was law. The judge never questioned a single action; it was a brilliant call. Despite Mellon's innate financial genius, which would propel him to incalculable wealth and national fame, Frick was the dominant personality in their lifelong friendship. For Frick it was always: "Andy." For A. W. it was invariably: "Mr. Frick." In 1880 Frick invited A. W. on a four-person trip to Europe. He had a twofold purpose. The trip helped him cement his relationship with Pittsburgh's

most important if not biggest banker. Mellon's money was always a little greener than the competition; it added cache. Accompanying them was A. A. Hutchinson, a Connellsville coke operator. Before the trip ended, Hutchinson, enchanted by the charms of Europe, agreed to sell out to Frick.

A. W. performed another very important service for Frick. He introduced him to his future wife. Or, more accurately, we should say he tried and failed. Attending a reception in June of 1881 with Mellon, Frick inquired about a tall slender woman with blue eyes and a soft smile. Mellon knew her; she was Adelaide Childs, the daughter of Asa P. Childs, the recently deceased shoe manufacturer and supplier to Frick's Broad Ford company store. Frick asked Mellon for an introduction. Bowing to the etiquette of the day, Mellon set off in search of an older guest to properly officiate. It took a little time. Meanwhile the aggressive Frick, panting and pacing like a bull in a far corner of a pasture, beat a beeline to Miss Childs and performed the duty himself. Mellon was probably relieved.

Doubtless 1881 was the most fateful year in Frick's life. He and Adelaide were married on December 15 and honeymooned in New York. There he met Andrew Carnegie for the first time. Carnegie and his forceful mother, Margaret, hosted a lunch for the newlyweds. At this lunch a second betrothal was solemnized. This time Frick sold him what was ultimately to be a controlling interest in H. C. Frick. Flush with the glow of the moment, Carnegie proclaimed: "It will be a great thing for Mr. Frick." Somewhat suspicious of the hard-driving Frick, Margaret Carnegie in her thick Scottish brogue, chimed in: "Tha is a verra good thing for Mr. Freek but Andra what will be the gain to oos." Afterward, Adelaide Frick received a beautiful bouquet from Carnegie. Frick urged her to write him a note. The note was never sent; Frick had sent the flowers.

Motivations on both sides bear some scrutiny. The Carnegie interests consumed large quantities of coke at both

the Lucy furnaces and at Edgar Thompson (E.T.), and they also produced coke themselves. At E.T. they had the lowest cost rail mill in the world. The same could not be said of their coke operations. It was common knowledge that the "coke king" was a low cost producer as well as the most knowledgeable and dominant figure in the business. Through pushing on the part of his brother Tom and his longtime partner Henry Phipps, Carnegie concluded that to fulfill his vision as the "king of steel" he must be an integrated producer—that is, control his own sources of raw material.

Frick's motives in hitching his already ascending star to Carnegie are less clear but we may hazard some guesses. Frick's ownership of the H. C. Frick Coke Company moved in teeter-totter fashion with the increase in ownership on the part of the Carnegie interests: in 1882, Frick 29.6 percent, Carnegie 11.25 percent; in 1885, Frick 16.7 percent, Carnegie 50.0 percent; and in 1888, Frick 21 percent, Carnegie 73.5 percent. From 1883 on Frick was not a controlling owner but an employee. Three lines of thought seem to have driven Frick into the Carnegie orbit, leaving behind the fierce independence his nature demanded.

First, with Frick it was not all about money. With Carnegie it was simple: make the money and then give it away. Both these efforts were inspired by genius. With Frick there were wider concerns—family, friends, art. The voluble Carnegie was at heart a loner. Frick was part of a social ecosystem. Second, Frick too shared Carnegie's vision of an integrated steel industry; there would ultimately be no coke king, only a steel king: Carnegie. Lastly, and perhaps most importantly, Frick was supremely confident in his ability to manage a vast enterprise. Despite being the "smartest man in the room," Carnegie was never a hands-on manager. Frick knew he would be indispensable before Carnegie found it out.

Frick's relationship with the man who would ulti-
mately control his destiny was contentious from the start.
The Connellsville seam occupied only 150 square miles.
Opportunities were limited, and prices were going up. Frick
moved boldly to consolidate the dominant position of the H. C.
Frick Coke Company. In 1883 when Carnegie opposed a Frick
coal acquisition, Frick was characteristically blunt. "I am free to
say, I do not like the tone of your letter. . . . In the matter of the
properties in question . . . I shall have to differ from you and I
think the future will bear me out." Carnegie backed down.

The coal fields had a long history of labor violence,
and early in his career Frick used strike breakers and private
police to crush any union activity. To the end of his life Frick
was antiunion in every fiber of his body. In 1887 H. C. Frick
Coke Company and the Syndicate of Coke Operators were
determined to suppress the striking mine workers as they had
done in the past. It was not to be. Early in 1886 Carnegie pub-
lished his "Triumphant Democracy," and in it he supported
the right of working men to organize. To enhance his image
as an enlightened capitalist and perhaps to keep his furnaces
going, he forced Frick to capitulate. Perhaps he perceived
Frick as a threat and determined to take him down a peg or
two. In any event Frick responded quickly; he resigned and
set off for Europe. Carnegie beseeched him to return and
before long he did. Frick had drawn a line in the sand, and
Carnegie would not dare to cross it for some time to come.

In addition to his strained relationship with Carnegie,
Frick suffered two other tragedies. In 1891 his six-year-old
daughter Martha succumbed as a result of a small pin she
had ingested at age two. The memory of Martha haunted
Adelaide and Frick for all the days of their lives. They blamed
themselves.

Frick did not blame himself (publicly at least) for the
Johnstown flood, although, rounding up the principal sus-

pects, Frick was clearly first in line. In 1878 Frick, along with a tunnel contractor, Benjamin Ruff, purchased an abandoned reservoir seventy miles northeast of Pittsburgh. They solicited fourteen other members for the exclusive South Fork Fishing and Hunting Club. Frick was the largest shareholder and a member of the executive committee. On May 31, 1889, a patently inadequate dam gave way sending twenty million tons of water, in some places seventy feet high, smashing into Johnstown—two thousand people lost their lives. It was the third greatest natural disaster in American history. We must not single out Frick in this tragedy. The elite of Pittsburgh doubtless shared a collective culpability. One can only imagine, in this "golden age of the plaintiffs bar," what civil and criminal liabilities might have been imposed. For better or worse it was a different age. One might be reminded of a line in F. Scott Fitzgerald's *The Great Gatsby*: "They were careless people Tom and Daisy—they smashed up things and creatures and then retreated back into their money or their vast carelessness . . . and then let other people clean up the mess."

Tom Carnegie died an early death in 1886. Despite a drinking problem he did yeoman service as Andrew Carnegie's right-hand man at Carnegie Brothers. Of equal importance he served as the lubricant that separated any "metal to metal" contact between Frick and his brother. Henry Phipps was given the chairmanship but he was a reluctant CEO and gradually deferred important decisions to Frick. Frick's June 1886 resignation caught both Carnegie and Phipps flat-footed. Despite Frick's prickly personality Carnegie knew he was indispensable to running H. C. Frick and for his leadership of the Connellsville Coke Syndicate. Furthermore, Carnegie sensed that he was becoming indispensable to the success of the burgeoning Carnegie steel interests. He was the only man who could ride the tiger. After a five-month European hiatus he was back on the job in November 1887.

Phipps passed more and more steel responsibilities onto Frick's willing shoulders. He lobbied Carnegie to have the rising star take his place and in January 1889 Frick was named chairman of Carnegie Brothers. This time around he was playing a stronger hand and he soon let Carnegie know it: "I cannot stand fault finding and I must feel that I have the entire confidence of the power that put me where I am. . . . I know I can manage both Carnegie Brothers and Frick Coke successfully." Carnegie was conciliatory: "Now I only want to know how your hand can be strengthened."

Frick not only squeezed efficiency and profits out of coke and steel; he also acted strategically. When a startup E.T. competitor at Duquesne, adjacent to Homestead, struggled, Frick used predatory pricing to force a sale to Carnegie at a bargain basement price of $1 million in long-term bonds. The deal was a home run and Carnegie was elated. In fact so confident was he in Frick's capabilities that at long last he merged Carnegie Brothers (E.T.) with Carnegie Phipps (Homestead) into the newly named Carnegie Steel in June of 1892.

Back in 1886 Frick had proposed to Carnegie that he transfer a significant portion of his H. C. Frick ownership for shares in Carnegie Brothers. Carnegie advised Frick not to take this step and then turned down his request. Later that year, after Frick returned from his "sabbatical" Carnegie changed his mind and granted him shares valued at $184,000 to be paid out of the share dividends. Further grants were made in 1888, 1890, and 1891, and, finally, in 1892 upon assuming the chairmanship of Carnegie Steel, his ownership rose to 11 percent and was equal to that of Carnegie's longtime partner Henry Phipps.

Frick's name will forever be linked to the infamous Homestead strike in the summer of 1892. Much of this opprobrium is well deserved; some of it is not. Labor violence in the coal fields was simply a way of life. Coal mining is a dirty, dan-

gerous, and, in those days, low-paying job. Unions were weak to nonexistent and would not be a viable counterweight to capital until the 1930s. There was a familiar pattern to coal country labor problems. Business conditions worsened, wages were cut, minors struck, replacement workers were hired, violence ensued, and private police or the state militia would quell the unrest. As the head of H. C. Frick and the de facto leader of the industry, Frick was antiunion to the core; he was unflinching. The one exception was 1887 when Carnegie's prolabor posturing pulled the rug out from under him. The miners struck again in 1891. It was the worst labor insurrection in the history of the H. C. Frick Coke Company. This time Carnegie did not interfere; events followed the usual pattern and Frick broke the strike. Twenty-five thousand men were on strike, forty-three were wounded, and eleven were killed. In several metrics the strike was more violent than Homestead.

When the Carnegie interests purchased the Homestead works of an undercapitalized competitor they inherited a union: the Amalgamated Association of Iron and Steel Workers. Frick had but one objective in dealing with the labor situation at Homestead in 1892. There was no negotiation; there was only a diktat. He intended to break the union.

Events proceeded in rapid succession. On July 1 he locked out the unionized workforce; on July 6 he barged three hundred Pinkertons up the Monongahela River, ostensibly to guard the plant, but in reality to facilitate the safe passage of replacement workers—scabs. All hell broke loose. The Pinkertons were rebuffed, and both guards and strikers were killed. These traumatic events were called out in banner headlines across the United States and Europe. Frick played the heavy. Carnegie had gone to Europe in June (exactly where Frick wanted him) and did not return until early 1893. Privately he supported Frick to the hilt despite his posturing about deep feelings for the working man. The implication

was that had he, Carnegie, been on the spot things would have been amicably settled. Any fair weighing of the facts surrounding Homestead leads to the conclusion that Frick acted far more honorably than Carnegie. The latter did not set a high bar. On July 12, eight thousand National Guard troops secured the plant. Replacement workers drifted in, and by November the strike was over. Charles Schwab was moved over from E.T., and by 1900 Homestead was the largest of the Carnegie mills and the largest steel plant in the world, with production of over two million tons of steel annually.

One of the most bizarre incidents in U.S. labor and industrial history occurred on Saturday, July 23, when a Russian anarchist, Alexander Berkman, attempted to assassinate Frick. While Frick was conferring with Carnegie Vice President John Leishman, Berkman burst into the office and fired a bullet that penetrated Frick's neck and lodged in the middle of his back. Leishman grabbed Berkman, who then got off a second shot, this time finding its home in Frick's neck. Berkman's third shot missed its victim. Frick then recovered and grabbed on to Berkman and along with Leishman spun around the office in a macabre dance. Frick, suffering from loss of blood, pulled the trio to the floor. A carpenter named Andy then entered the room and began to beat Berkman on the head with a hammer. Berkman was a slight man, no bigger than Frick. Despite being outnumbered and beaten on the head, Berkman managed to pull a stiletto out of his pocket and drive it into Frick's back, hip, right side, and left leg.

The police finally arrived and Berkman was subdued but he was not finished. He was chewing something—it was not Wrigley's Spearmint. In his mouth was a capsule of fulminate of mercury of sufficient strength to blow the entire building apart. Despite two bullets and four stab wounds, Frick maintained his consciousness. When a doctor arrived and started to

give Frick anesthetic he refused, preferring to guide the doctor toward the two imbedded bullets. Smiling wanly, he commented: "Don't make it too bad doctor for I must be at the office on Monday." It took the doctor two hours to locate and extract the two bullets, and then, defying all reason or common sense, Frick returned to his work where he left off. He remained at it an hour or so as if he had only dozed off and had a bad dream. Hemingway had a phrase for this kind of courage, he called it: "grace under pressure." Rightfully, Frick was universally lauded for his superhuman performance. Through no fault of its own the Amalgamated lost much of its public support. Berkman's bullet never found Frick's heart but did penetrate the heart of the Homestead strike.

The Carnegie/Frick defeat of labor at Homestead cleared the way for spectacular profit growth from under $2 million in 1893 to almost $40 million in 1900. The reputations of both men were damaged by the strike—Carnegie's more so than Frick's. As the success of the company and the size of the Carnegie fortune advanced in tandem, Carnegie was of two minds. He recognized and valued Frick's exceptional capabilities, but at the same time he resented Frick's growing reputation and the power he had so willingly delegated to the Carnegie chairman.

During the years 1893 and 1894 he ramped up his meddling in Frick's management of the steel and coke companies. Frick sought to purchase a portion of Henry Oliver's Mesabi ore properties. Carnegie was vocal in opposition: "Oliver's ore bargain is just like him—nothing in it." Frick forged ahead anyway and eventually extended their ore holdings with leases from John D. Rockefeller. Perennial violence in the coal fields again flared, resulting in the murder of J. H. Paddock, the chief engineer of the coke company. Carnegie, writing from Scotland, was unsympathetic. During competitive bidding for a Russian armor contract, Carnegie disclosed

the bid price and lost the business to Bethlehem Steel. The straw that broke the camel's back was Carnegie's decision to merge the works of independent coal operator W. S. Rainey into H. C. Frick Coke. Frick was not consulted. He resigned in December 1894.

As he usually did, Carnegie backpedaled but this time to no avail. John G. A. Leishman was made president, and, through the intervention of Henry Phipps, Frick agreed to take the position of non-executive chairman. For two years this arrangement worked well. Leishman handled the day-to-day activities and most of the interface with Carnegie, while Frick continued to call all the major shots. But after two years Leishman made some indiscreet personal investments, and in March of 1897 he was replaced by Charles Schwab. Frick facilitated this switch, and for him it was an improvement over the quite satisfactory arrangement with Leishman. Schwab was an incomparably better manager than Leishman and was destined to succeed Frick as the full-fledged CEO of Carnegie Steel. Schwab was young (thirty-five), and Frick had brought him along every step of the way. "Smilin' Charlie," as he was known, had other talents that served both himself and the enterprise. He had superb political skills and mediated between the prickly Frick and the mercurial Carnegie as nobody else could.

As both Frick and Carnegie grew increasingly comfortable with Schwab's leadership of Carnegie Steel, the day of Frick's permanent exit grew closer. The fatal year was 1899. Carnegie indicated by vague language, as always, that he was amenable to a buyout. He granted Frick and Phipps an option for $1,170,000, of which the final $170,000 came from the two Carnegie partners. They could not arrange the financing and Carnegie gleefully pocketed their option money.

The final break occurred over coke prices. Carnegie insisted upon a price of $1.35 per ton, while Frick moved

prices steadily up as the market strengthened to $1.75 a ton. Two reasonable men could have settled on a middling figure, but Frick and Carnegie had no desire to be reasonable. They only shared in common a mutual desire to be rid of one another. On December 5, 1899 Carnegie called for Frick's resignation at a board meeting in Pittsburgh. Without a fuss Frick resigned. But Carnegie was not through. Having stripped Frick of his power he then attempted to deprive him of the better part of his wealth. His weapon of choice was the "iron clad agreement." This was the brainchild of Henry Phipps and was drafted in 1877 shortly after the death of Tom Carnegie. It provided that a partner's share could be purchased at book value (far below the fair market value) from his estate with payments over time. This was designed to prevent a forced liquidation of the company. A second clause of particular importance to the Frick/Carnegie struggle provided that a partner could be forced to sell his shares back to the company at book value upon a 75% vote of the shareholders. Carnegie got the required signatures and Frick was offered $5 million for his shares. On Carnegie's part it was an unconscionable act. Frick threatened to sue, making public the fantastic profitability of Carnegie Steel. The consequences could have been dire. With the intercession again of Henry Phipps (who, to his credit, refused to vote with Carnegie) and other mutual friends, Carnegie backed down. Frick walked away with a nice step up to $31 million ($620 million in today's money). Things only got better for Frick in 1901 upon the sale of Carnegie Steel to the newly formed Morgan-backed United States Steel Corporation. His holdings were valued at $61.4 million ($1.228 billion).

At the time of the formation of U.S. Steel in 1901, Frick was fifty-two and at the height of his powers. Had he been asked to run the giant corporation he would doubtless have done so, but the call never came—Carnegie may have had

something to do with it. He did serve as a director and member of the powerful finance committee until his death in 1919. Elbert H. Gary, U.S. Steel's longstanding chairman, said of Frick: "He spoke little . . . and said much."

After his move to New York in 1902, Frick left behind a career as an industrial manager and assumed the mantle of a national finance capitalist of the first rank. He soon became a director of National City Bank, Equitable Life Assurance Company, and several other major corporations. Even more important were his ties to the major railroads. He was a director of the Chicago and Northwestern, Union Pacific, Atchison Topeka and Santa Fe, B&O, Norfolk Western, and the fabled Pennsylvania railroads. He had at one time or another $6 million invested in each of these roads.

Frick did not forget about Pittsburgh. In 1899 he joined A. W. Mellon in the formation of the Union Trust Company, and in 1902 joined the board of Mellon National Bank, the successor to T. Mellon & Sons. By 1906 Frick was the largest property holder in Pittsburgh. His two signature developments in downtown Pittsburgh still grace Grant Street: the Frick Building and the William Penn Hotel.

Since the age of thirty Frick had been collecting art. With somewhat more time and a great deal more money after 1901, he set about building one of the nation's great and enduring collections. In 1914 he completed a sixty-room mansion at 5th Avenue and 70th Street in Manhattan. It was designed to serve as a permanent repository for the Frick art collection. At his death it held works by El Greco, Gainsborough, Goya, Hals, Millet, Monet, Rembrandt, Rubens, Turner, Velázquez, Van Dyck, Veronese, and Whistler.

Frick died in 1919 at the age of seventy, four months after his partner and nemesis Carnegie. He left an estate of $145 million ($2.9 billion in today's money). $117 million or 5/6 was directed toward charitable good works. Art valued at

$50 million plus a $15 million endowment went to establish a museum open to the public at One 70th Street. Fifteen million dollars went to Princeton (where his son Childs was educated) and $5 million each to Harvard and MIT. Pittsburgh received the 151-acre Frick Park and later bequests through his daughter Helen. Money also went to the coke region.

Frick is not an easy man to come to terms with. Beyond doubt he is a seminal figure in the emergence of the steel industry and indeed industrial America. Within steel he stands second only to Carnegie, and one can easily give him preeminence by arguing that Carnegie was not a steel man but rather a financier and promoter—without parallel.

His charitable endeavors merit the highest praise. At $117 million ($2.34 billion in today's dollars) they dwarf Heinz and Westinghouse, and as a percentage of his estate they exceed the bequests of his friend A. W. Mellon. Andrew Carnegie was a beloved figure; he worked at it. He never missed an opportunity at every stage of his career to burnish his reputation and place in history. Frick did not. If we ask his doppelganger why not, we might hear an echo of Clark Gable's last line in *Gone With the Wind*: "Frankly . . . I don't give a damn."

6

THE JUDGE AND THE LITTLE BOY: THE TRIUMPH AND TRAGEDY OF A. W. MELLON

THE YEAR IS 1866. WITH MONOTONOUS REGULARITY AN older man and a little boy boarded the train in East Liberty for the short run downtown. The older man, formally attired in a long-tailed frock coat and a high-starched wing collar, spoke to the boy about matters of consequence; he spoke to him as an adult. The boy volunteers little; in rapt attention he seems to absorb rather than listen. The older man was Judge Thomas Mellon (1813–1907). The boy was his third surviving son, Andrew William Mellon (1855–1937).

Thomas Mellon, an Ulster Scot—commonly called Scots Irish—came to the United States from Ireland in 1818 and settled with the extended Mellon family in Westmoreland County, Pennsylvania. Like young Henry Ford, farm life was not for him. He soon headed to nearby Pittsburgh for a college education and new opportunities. In 1827 he came upon a copy of Benjamin Franklin's "Autobiography." The book, which he read

A. W. Mellon. Courtesy of the Library of Congress

several times, left a stunning impression. Resolution, frugality, and industry would lead their devotee to wealth and prominence. Franklin's precepts melded comfortably with the Scots Irish Presbyterian doctrine of industry and self-reliance. All this formed a template that lasted not for one lifetime, but for two.

He graduated from the Western University of Pennsylvania (later the University of Pittsburgh) in 1837. He was better educated than any of his forebears and, by his own design, better than any of his offspring. He read law, not out of any love of the profession, but, lacking capital, law offered the best entry point into the world of business. Mortgages, foreclosures, real estate, and property development provided greater financial rewards than legal fees. The shift from law to business was slow but inexorable. Deals were small but he executed them flawlessly; his scope of operations grew. In 1843, he estimated his net worth at $12,000 ($300,000 in today's money). At age thirty he set out to find a wife.

Sarah Jane Negley was the daughter of Jacob Negley. The Negleys were one of the founding families of Pittsburgh, and

Jacob was the proud possessor of a 1500-acre estate with a mansion dominating his own little village in what is now the East Liberty section of Pittsburgh. The courtship of Sarah Jane was conducted with all the thoroughness of a military campaign. Mellon intended to marry up. He needed a wife of appropriate social status to buttress the fulfillment of his driving ambition. Money was not the decider, but it would help. Sarah Jane's share of the Negley estate was $50,000, roughly four times Mellon's net worth.

The courtship involved a seemingly endless series of visits to the Negley mansion. Sarah Jane was not swept off her feet, but eventually succumbed. Mellon describes the process in brutally frank terms in his 1885 autobiography: "There was no love beforehand so far as I was concerned. Nothing but a good opinion of worthy qualities; if I had been rejected I would have felt neither sad nor depressed only annoyed as to the loss of time." He chose well. Mellon and Sarah Jane lived in a house he built on her property at 401 Negley Avenue for fifty-seven years.

Eight children came in steady succession between 1844 and 1860. Two sets of boys survived to adulthood: Thomas A. (1844–1899), James Ross (1846–1934), Andrew W. (1855–1937), and Richard B. (1858–1933). The Mellon family, as directed by the Judge, was to be a financial unit much like the farming family that had been his provenance. The idea that each child would be educated to freely pursue his talents and desires—lawyer, doctor, scientist—the Judge would have none of it. There was one profession and one profession only for the Mellon boys: business. "I secured free admission to their confidence from the first and participated in all their plans; and in return incurred their willing cooperation in *my* purposes for their plans." His boys were to be extensions of himself both economically and personally (existentially). His was a multigenerational plan; his progeny and their stewardship of his fortune were to be his immortality. There was little

light or levity at 401 Negley; Thomas Mellon was a humorless, hard man.

Taking a lesson from Plato, the Judge started his own school at home. Not surprisingly the curriculum focused on the practical: reading, writing, and arithmetic. Poetry, literature, and even science had no place in Mellon's school. The older pair, Thomas A. and James Ross, was rushed into business and thus received considerably less education than their father. While still in their teens Thomas ran a nursery and James a coal mine; both were successful.

Mellon's fortune was built on real estate. Beginning with foreclosures he then moved into buying and selling small properties. He subdivided farmland near the city and took positions in coal properties. His sterling reputation in the law, buttressed by Sarah Jane's family connections, helped him expand the scope of his operations. While he turned his back on farming, property, whether in the form of mortgages, real estate, or minerals, provided the common thread in all his investments. A bolder, less cautious man might have turned to operating businesses. In midcentury Pittsburgh manufacturing was the obvious choice. Here money could be made many times faster than with the Judge's painstaking real assets investments—or it could be lost. For every Carnegie, Westinghouse, or Heinz there were thousands of failures and scores of also-rans.

The Anointed Son

In 1859 Mellon won election to the office of associate law judge in the Court of Common Pleas. He was, throughout the rest of his life, known as the "Judge." Relieved of the burdens of his law practice while enhancing his reputation and contacts through his judicial office, he devoted increasing time to building his already sizable fortune. But in the quest for fortune and prominence of the first rank he had fallen short; the money would simply not pile up fast enough. But

the Judge had a secret weapon: his sixth-born child, Andrew William Mellon. The Mellon story is one of a seamless connection between the Judge and the little boy.

Andrew's nearest sibling was Selwyn (1853–1862). The tragedy of Selwyn's early death weighed heavily upon young Andrew. It drew him closer to the Judge. With failing eyesight the Judge drafted Andrew to read to him the serious works in his intellectual diet. In Darwin, Spencer, and Huxley, Andrew read and absorbed the lessons of capitalism red of tooth and claw, as he and his father would understand it firsthand as practitioners. The Judge duly paid for these reading services at twenty-five cents per hour. He doubtless sensed the precociousness in Andrew and let his education run beyond that of his older brothers—but within bounds. Between 1869 and 1872 Andrew took a combined preparatory/college course at the Western University. He left without a degree. At the uncommunicative dinner table at 401 Negley, Andrew received top prize for silence; he always kept his own counsel. His character, set early on, was a contradictory amalgam of diffidence, inhibition, and shyness, coupled with powerful confidence and self-sufficiency. Despite the onslaughts of wealth, fame, and power this mold was never broken.

A few months after stepping down from the bench the Judge founded a private bank "T. Mellon & Sons" at 514 Smithfield Street. Two years later he erected a four-story iron-front building with a statue of the iconic Benjamin Franklin standing above the door. These premises remained the bank headquarters for the next fifty years.

During his time at Western University, Andrew spent every Saturday and time off from school at the bank. From 1872 on he was there full time. He absorbed the rhythms of the bank like a sponge. Determining that Andrew and his younger brother Dick needed some practical operating experience, the Judge set them up in a building supply business

similar to that run by Thomas and James in East Liberty. Andrew capably piloted the enterprise and returned to the bank just in time to stand by his father as they weathered the financial panic of 1873. T. Mellon & Sons survived, but the Judge was shaken and humiliated. He had to stop payments to most customers, and at one point nearly closed the bank. As an early indication of A. W.'s prescience, he felt the building supply business was too good in 1873, and leased the lumberyard to a competitor a few months before the crash. As the Judge declaimed: "A masterful stroke." At nineteen he was back full time at the bank. The Judge's growing confidence in Andrew, coupled with his failing eyesight, led to a change of the guard at T. Mellon & Sons. In early 1882, he turned it over, lock, stock, and barrel, to Andrew. The Judge was sixty-nine; Andrew twenty-seven. In the wake of 1873, it wasn't much: only modest profits and a very good name.

As the driving force at T. Mellon & Sons, A. W. was fast out of the chute. Less educated, less articulate, and far less of a commanding presence than his father, one might have expected a caretaker mentality on the part of the new proprietor, cautiously, carefully, and skillfully expanding the family fortune in the style of the Judge. But beneath that saturnine countenance brooded a white-hot flame of ambition equal to that of Carnegie. He inherited from his father the analytical skills of banking practice. But they provided only the foundation upon which rested vision, imagination, and clear appetite for risk. The Judge had long sensed there was a special quality in the little boy, but it is a fair guess that A. W.'s results far exceeded even his most sanguine projections.

One of the early customers at the new iron-front bank at 514 Smithfield was Henry Clay Frick (1849–1919). Frick was building his empire of beehive coke ovens in Fayette County, Pennsylvania. Battered by the storm of 1873 he was

stretched thin but sought to expand at the expense of his bankrupt competitors. The Judge made a series of loans that grew under his tenure to over $100,000. In 1876, at the end of a meeting with Frick, he introduced him to Andew. Frick was Andrew's senior by six years. He was better educated and much more a man of the world. Frick called him Andy, but Andy always referred to the coke king as Mr. Frick. They became good friends, as well as close business associates. Frick dominated the friendship, but the younger man's accomplishments would far outstrip those of "Mr. Frick."

In 1881, in partnership with Henry Frick, Mellon acquired control of the Pittsburgh National Bank of Commerce; in 1883 he bought the Union Insurance Company and started the Braddock Bank. In 1886, again with Frick, he founded the Fidelity Title & Trust Company. With a larger financial base he set his sights on the burgeoning industrial opportunities that Pittsburgh offered. Along with Colonel James M. Guffey, an inveterate oil prospector and promoter, he established and controlled the Westmoreland Carbon Gas Company and the Southwestern Pennsylvania Natural Gas Company. He was also a substantial investor in the Bridgewater Gas Company and the Shenango Valley Gas Company, and, while not destined to be a major Mellon enterprise, he financed John Pitcairn in the newly established Pittsburgh Plate Glass Company.

R. B. "Dick" Mellon joined T. Mellon & Sons as vice president in 1887. He became a full partner, pretty much splitting everything with his brother fifty-fifty. As A. W. described it: "It was an outright gift. . . . I just said to come in and he came in and we were partners." In 1890 and 1895 the Judge transferred virtually all of his assets to A. W., who managed them on behalf of his brothers until 1919. The appraised value of the Judge's estate was $2.5 million, and it was estimated that

the four boys possessed a like amount. In today's dollars the Mellon fortune in 1895 stood at $100 million.

Aluminum

Although he made more money in oil, A. W. always allowed that his favorite investment was aluminum. In 1889, Captain Alfred Ephraim Hunt and two young associates, Arthur Vining Davis and George Clapp, presented themselves at 514 Smithfield seeking $4,000 for their struggling Pittsburgh Reduction Company. Their prospects hinged upon the patents of a young Oberlin College graduate, Charles Martin Hall, for the electrolytic reduction of aluminum from bauxite. The company was small, the technology still questionable, and the team, with the exception of Captain Hunt, a veteran steel metallurgist, was yet unproven. It was a classic venture capital investment long before the term had been invented. It was an investment the Judge would never have listened to, let alone made.

The wolf was clearly at the door for the Pittsburgh Reduction Company (later Alcoa). It might well have been no Mellon, no Alcoa. A. W. knew and respected Captain Hunt. The technology seemed feasible, but there were doubts. In the end it was Davis who won him over. Davis, twenty-two years old with a pimento loaf complexion and waxed ibex-horn mustaches, was soon monopolizing the conversation: "I'll tell you the worst. I am a college graduate (Amherst) and the son of a minister but I mean to pay." Mellon was sold. Knowing the crew would never make it on $4,000, he offered $25,000 to provide much-needed working capital. In venture capital as in a horserace, technology is the horse, management is the jockey and the market is the track. Alcoa rang the bell on all three counts.

There were losses, lawsuits, tariff issues, and a host of problems scaling an entire new industry. The bank advanced

more money and A. W. joined the board, followed soon by R. B. They were diligent directors, working with the company every step of the way for many years. While very influential, they never controlled Alcoa. In 1894 their stake was 12 percent. With Arthur Vining Davis, A. W. had judged well. Forty years after his initial investment Mellon recalled: "For a great many years I depended entirely on Mr. Davis. . . . You might say he was practically the entire business."

Oil

Aluminum is big business; oil is the biggest business. The Mellons got into oil by fits and starts. Robert Fulton Galey, the Judge's old friend, convinced him to take a small position in a few wells along the Clarion River—the sums were modest and the wells soon petered out; the Judge didn't like oil or oil prospectors.

By 1889 there were numerous oil strikes near Pittsburgh. A. W.'s nephew, William Larimer Mellon (1868–1949), was at the bank and eager to be a hands-on operator. John Galey (Robert's son) fired his imagination, and the two of them convinced A. W. and R. B. to give them backing. They had more confidence in young W. L., or Willie as they called him, than they did Galey. Success followed; money was advanced. The more success they had the more money they needed. Gathering lines were built to bring the crude to Coraopolis where it was sold to Rockefeller's Standard Oil.

They then built a refinery and began to sell refined products in competition with Standard Oil. The business grew, offshore markets beckoned, and soon the Crescent Oil Company (35 percent A. W., 35 percent R. B., and 30 percent W. L.) owned four hundred tank cars that carried the oil east. They had baited the bear, and Standard took action. The Pennsylvania Railroad, at the behest of Standard Oil, imposed crippling rates upon the Mellon enterprise. The

Mellons counterattacked by building a 271-mile pipeline from Pittsburgh to Marcus Hook on the Delaware River. Standard Oil and the Pennsylvania Railroad threw up legal roadblocks at every step of the way. However, Pennsylvania was the Mellons' home turf; they had friends in high places. The pipeline went through. It was the only pipeline in Pennsylvania not controlled by Standard Oil. They now had an integrated oil company with a refinery on the Delaware River.

By 1895 the Mellons were reputedly shipping 10 percent (probably high) of the nation's oil exports. They had invested $2.5 million in Crescent, far and away the biggest investment they had ever made. They knew when to fold. In 1895 they sold the company to Standard Oil for $4.5 million; 30 percent went to W. L. and the rest to his uncles on Smithfield Street. The profits were good, and they took no little pride in having bested the mighty Standard Oil Company.

Act three of Mellon's oil investments began in 1900. The same inveterate prospectors and promoters who had previously led Mellon to oil caught A. W.'s ear again, and he backed them in a well at Spindletop, Texas. Spindletop spewed forth oil at a phenomenal rate of forty thousand barrels a day. It was the biggest gusher the nascent oil industry had ever seen. This operation was far bigger than Crescent and it took far more money. The Mellons were on the oil treadmill once again. They laid pipelines, built a refinery at Port Arthur, Texas, and bought a fleet of tankers to service distribution nodes in several East Coast cities. Problems abounded—too much oil, narrowed profit margins, and Guffey, a genius at finding oil, was a lousy manager. A. W. headed for the exits. Along with W. L. he went to New York and approached Standard Oil. Their unpleasant experience in the losing battle with Mellon over Crescent was fresh in their minds; they turned him down.

When you can't go backward you've got to go forward. A. W. upped the stakes. He sent W. L. to Texas, just as a major

new field was opening near Tulsa, Oklahoma. Standard again was the team to beat. As luck would have it, in November of 1906, Theodore Roosevelt pulled the trigger on the historic antitrust suit against Standard Oil. With little obstruction this time, they built a pipeline four hundred miles from Tulsa to Port Arthur. They pushed Guffey out and W. L. built a team capable of running a now-sizable business.

Gulf Oil, as one of the seven sister international oil companies, became the crown jewel of the Mellon empire. In 1928 Gulf's net assets were $650 million. A. W., R. B., and W. L. held 70 percent of the stock in the still-private Gulf Oil Company, the largest company ever to come out of Pittsburgh. Even on a lengthy laundry list of major Mellon investments, Gulf probably accounted for 40 percent of the family fortune. Reflecting back upon his turndown by the Standard, the laconic A. W. remarked: "They weren't so smart, were they?"

Halcyon Days

In 1895, Edward G. Acheson, a protégé of Thomas Edison, presented himself at 514 Smithfield Street. He offered a thumb-sized sample of silicon made ultra hard by heavy doses of electricity. Mellon applied this new material to a facet of his diamond ring, producing a scratch. You see, Acheson proclaimed: "It takes a diamond to cut a diamond." It was a smaller reprise of his Alcoa experience. Mellon smiled; he was in. Unfortunately for Acheson's dreams but fortunately for the Mellons' original stake, Acheson proved to be no Arthur Vining Davis. The company was moved to Niagara Falls for cheap power. Acheson proved to be a lackadaisical and inept manager. Losses followed. A. W. replaced Acheson with his long-time Pittsburgh associate Frank W. Haskell. Further investments stabilized the company and gave the Mellons control. The Carborundum Company would grow to

become the world's foremost producer of grinding and abrasive material.

In 1900, W. L. introduced engineer inventors Howard H. W. McClintic and Charles D. Marshall to his uncle. They proposed a steel fabricating company, targeting large projects. Background checks proved out; however, his frequent partner, Frick, told A. W.: "Don't touch it." They needed $100,000 and A. W. agreed to do half. Gloom clouded their faces as the young engineers confessed they didn't have $50,000. Mellon offered some suggestions: "How about loans from your parents or a mortgage on your houses? Your reluctance leads me to believe you lack faith in your enterprise." Amid furtive glances at one another they agreed to mortgage their homes. Mellon was only probing. "My brother and I will loan you the additional money." They should have taken out the mortgages. McClintic Marshall went on to become the largest steel fabricator in the world, raising a long list of iconic projects including the George Washington Bridge, Grand Central Station, and the locks on the Panama Canal. In 1931 the company was sold to Bethlehem Steel. The brothers split $40 million.

While Gulf, Alcoa, Carborundum, McClintic Marshall, and the bank proved the core of Mellon holdings, A. W. at the same time financed a bewildering variety of small stones to surround these crown jewels. Most of these investments were made in a veritable cyclone of activity in a two-year period bracketing 1900.

In 1899, in concert with Frick and W. H. Donner, the former head of Cambria Iron Works, they founded the Union Steel Company. At a site near Donora, south of Monessen, they erected an integrated steel mill to produce wire products. In 1900, again with Frick, they founded the New York Shipbuilding Company at Camden, New Jersey. That same year he financed the Union Steel Company, to consolidate

a number of Pittsburgh-area specialty steel producers. Along with Henry Oliver and Frick, Mellon launched the Standard Steel Car Company in 1902. With its flamboyant super-salesman "Diamond Jim" Brady, it was flooded with orders and was a hit right from the start. A. W. and R. B. soon became the controlling shareholders. In 1929 it was sold to the Pullman Company for $39 million. W. L. was in for 6 percent.

Mellon investments were not all confined to Pittsburgh. A. W. was a major investor in the Trade Dollar Consolidating Mining Company with silver mines in Idaho. From 1895 on, it poured out a cornucopia of cash, which helped finance the many Mellon enterprises that were early on cash consumers. Closer to home, in 1899, A. W. launched the Monongahela River Coal Company and the Pittsburgh Coal Company. Together they controlled 11 percent of U.S. coal production. There were few major investments after 1902.

One notable exception was the Koppers Company. Heinrich Koppers, a German, developed a by-product method of coke production to replace the beehive ovens upon which Frick had built his fortune. By-product coke was the coming thing. The gaseous by-products were not vented into the atmosphere but recycled to produce a variety of valuable chemicals, most notably benzene and toluene. The Mellons took a stake of 37 percent in 1915. When the United States entered the war, chemical prices went through the roof. Heinrich Koppers's 20 percent holding was seized by the U.S. government, and A. W. and R. B. wound up with 55 percent. Koppers went on to become a Fortune 500 company.

A few big ones got away. In 1890 George Westinghouse sought a $500,000 loan. A. W. insisted on a sizable equity stake and the right to name key Westinghouse managers. Westinghouse said "no" and went to New York. Had Mellon given Westinghouse the same flexibility he gave to Davis at Alcoa he would have secured a major stake in what would

eventually become the thirteenth largest industrial company in the United States. In 1899, after Frick and major Carnegie shareholder Henry Phipps failed in an effort to buy Carnegie Steel, Mellon negotiated directly with the wily Carnegie. While Mellon was organizing his syndicate Carnegie sold to J. P. Morgan. Years later Mellon confided to a young Frank Denton: "Carnegie double-crossed me."

A reasonable estimate of the combined worth of the Mellon family in 1900 would be $5 million ($100 million in today's dollars). A decade later this number had probably increased twenty-fold. How did A. W. Mellon do it? The Judge once said that it might be a good thing if Andy lost a loan; virtually without exception it never happened.

A. W. Mellon was a superb banker and a keen judge of character. Successful entrepreneurs are committed body and soul to the propagation of their enterprise. They are duly cautious but not normally skeptical. Carnegie and Westinghouse are prime examples. As F. Scott Fitzgerald observed, the test of a first-rate mind is to hold two opposing ideas in equipoise. Thus skepticism and unwavering commitment are at the heart of A. W. Mellon's genius. The other distinguishing feature of the Mellon system was its reliance on family. As A. W. and the Judge were of a piece, so were A. W., R. B., and their nephew W. L.—only ten years younger than R. B. W. L. was indispensable in the success of Gulf Oil and contributed to a host of other Mellon investments. R. B. was well fed, well balanced, and jovial. In the critical interviews with the entrepreneurs who sought Mellon support, he skillfully filled the gaping holes in the conversation as his brother silently calculated the likely outcomes. Perhaps more importantly he provided his psychologically fragile brother with crucial emotional support. In the end, A. W. pulled the trigger on every deal—no A. W., no vast Mellon fortune. But in the absence of R. B., it is

reasonable to doubt whether A. W. could have sustained the effort.

Disaster

To describe A. W.'s marriage as an unmitigated disaster is being charitable. R. B. married in 1897, leaving his brother a middle-aged bachelor, still at 401 Negley, taking silent dinners with his parents. On a crossing to Europe in 1898, Frick introduced Mellon to Nora McMullen, nineteen, the youngest of nine children and the only daughter. Her father was a brewer and gentleman farmer. A. W. visited the McMullens briefly and returned the next year to propose. With wisdom beyond her years, Nora turned him down: "You must see it is a mistake. . . . It would mean nothing but unhappiness for us both." When A. W. persisted the Judge weighed in: "Don't marry an English girl, Andy. . . . Their way of life is different than ours." Casting aside prudent advice and common sense, A. W. won the prize and they were married in 1900.

What was wrong with this marriage? Just about everything: a twenty-four-year age difference, her life *was* different, grimy Pittsburgh versus the English countryside, character defects, bad behavior. . . . Her list of sins is long, but, in her defense, she was young and her instincts argued against the marriage. Mellon's aggressiveness smashed through every roadblock posted by common sense. When the newlyweds departed the train at East Liberty, Nora exclaimed: "We don't get off here, do we? You don't live here." From here the marriage only went downhill. The mystique of his wealth aside, A. W. Mellon was poor marriage material; he was consumed by business and was just embarking on his most productive decade. It would have taken a very even-tempered and understanding woman to accommodate herself to A. W.'s very fixed lifestyle.

Just a year after their marriage and the birth of their daughter Ailsa, Nora developed a romantic interest in an

Englishman, Alfred Curphey. Here was a villain right out of a nineteenth-century melodrama. Curphey, still married, had squandered his wife's moderate means and was looking for ripe pickings. With Nora he hit the jackpot. For openers he came to Pittsburgh, talked Mellon into a $20,000 loan, and took up an extended residence at Mellon's Forbes Street home. He soon began squiring Nora around Pittsburgh during A. W.'s business travels. By 1903, on an ostensible visit to England, she took up residence with Curphey. In 1904 she told A. W. she wanted a divorce and intended to live with Curphey in England.

Mellon, determined to hang on, secured a promise from Curphey to forget Nora for 20,000 pounds. This bought Mellon sufficient time to see his son Paul born in 1907. The situation continued to worsen. Having squandered his Mellon payoff, Curphey reunited with Nora in 1908. She beseeched A. W. for a regular allowance. A. W. offered $10,000; Nora insisted on $20,000 ($500,000 in today's money), most of it earmarked for Curphey. In 1909 Nora renewed her 1904 demand for a divorce. Mellon sought middle ground with a separation. He offered to provide Nora with the income from a $600,000 trust fund as well as an initial payment of $250,000. Ailsa and Paul were to be shuttled back and forth between the parents, but with the explicit understanding they were never to see Curphey in Nora's presence. By December of 1909 the children were in Paris with Nora and Curphey. Things came to a head in 1910. Nora was required to see Ailsa and Paul only in Pittsburgh and move back into the Forbes Street home; Mellon moved out.

The situation was intolerable and Mellon filed for divorce on the grounds of adultery. The McMullen family, including Nora's mother, was firmly on the Mellon's side. In Pennsylvania a divorce on the grounds of adultery called for a jury trial with all the attendant risks of an unfavorable verdict and

adverse publicity. As it turned out, the Mellon divorce provided enough scandal to fill a year's worth of *National Enquirer* covers.

Mellon then called in his political chips and had the Pennsylvania legislature pass a law providing for a private hearing with a judge. This, of itself, created a storm of publicity, still leaving Mellon the difficult task of proving adultery. To that end he hired an army of operatives spanning out over Europe to obtain supporting testimony. Through a combination of prior efforts on behalf of Nora and Curphey to cover their tracks, third-rate gumshoes, and plain bad luck, he came up empty. Nora fought back. She ceaselessly, and with some degree of success, poisoned the minds of Ailsa and Paul against their father. In a scorching interview in a Philadelphia paper Norma described A. W.'s suit against her as: "Gold fighting against one lone woman. [Gold] may take my babies from me." This was Nora's answer to William Jennings Bryan's *Cross of Gold* speech. For Mellon it was the worst nightmare of his life. In the end Mellon won a pyrrhic victory of sorts. The children were to remain in Pittsburgh, with Nora allowed four months' visiting rights.

The kindest thing to be said about A. W.'s marriage to Nora may be: "'Tis better to have loved and lost than never to have loved at all." But, given the resulting human carnage, one must wonder. Mellon took the pain to his grave, and Ailsa and Paul were badly scarred. They suffered the most.

National Figure
Following the pattern set by the Judge, Mellon sought political influence to further his business interests. With his burgeoning empire playing out on the national stage, Mellon became one of the biggest donors to the Republican Party. In 1920 Pennsylvania's two senators, Philander Knox (a longtime confidant of A. W.) and Boise Penrose, lobbied President-Elect Warren G. Harding to name A. W. secretary

of the Treasury. He needed a change; his great creative period as a businessman had ended ten years earlier. The second highest position in the cabinet would help fill the aching void in his life.

Upon his succession to the Treasury he resigned sixty-three directorships. Dick Mellon became the go-to guy for all the Mellon enterprises; he performed admirably. Nonetheless, A. W. was only a phone call away, and the brothers frequently consulted on important matters. A. W. never hesitated to use his considerable influence on behalf of the Mellon empire. He would actively lobby Congress on behalf of Gulf Oil and Alcoa. It was a different world then.

A. W. Mellon's eleven-year tenure at the Treasury under three presidents—Harding, Coolidge, and Hoover—from 1921 to 1932, was surpassed only by Albert Gallitan. Mellon was frequently referred to as the greatest Treasury secretary since Alexander Hamilton. When Coolidge declined to run in 1928, there was serious talk of Mellon for president. The country was riding high on a floodtide of prosperity. The world's most preeminent financier, both private and public, was at the helm. The Mellon presidential movement never got off the ground and it's doubtful that he had much interest. First, at seventy-three he was too old; second, one can hardly imagine Mellon out on the stump in the manner of Nelson Rockefeller at Coney Island, pressing the flesh in one hand while munching a hot dog with the other: "Hiya, fella." It was not to be.

Mellon's long tenure at the Treasury was a first-rate performance. The times were right for Mellon, and Mellon was right for the times. As Calvin Coolidge famously proclaimed: "The business of America is business." Mellon could not have said it better. Spending was cut, taxes were cut, and surpluses abounded; America and A. W. Mellon had become bankers to the world.

The crash came in 1929, followed by the Great Depression. Soon Mellon was at sea, and the entire Hoover administration was foundering. It is unfair to blame Mellon for the financial disaster that befell the country. The sources of the problem extend far back to the harshness of the 1919 Treaty of Versailles. What might have been a financial panic in the manner of 1893 or 1907 was dragged into a world-wide depression by Europe. In retrospect, Mellon had only old tools to deal with a new problem. His solution was what Hoover termed that of the "liquidation school." Mellon's answer: "Liquidate labor, liquidate stocks, liquidate the farmer, liquidate real estate." His time had passed. Hoover eased him out in February of 1932 by naming him ambassador to the Court of St. James.

Art and Philanthropy

A. W. Mellon was introduced to art by Frick in the late 1890s. His early purchases were inexpensive and undistinguished. Mellon deepened his interest in art around 1905, spending some $400,000 on a variety of good art but none that would eventually make it into the National Gallery. With the Mellon fortune in full flower after 1920, Mellon accelerated his purchases. This time he was guided by Joseph Duveen, to whom he had been introduced by the ever-present Frick. From 1923 on, with the aggressive and adroit Duveen pushing him along, Mellon became the most important art collector in the country. A dozen or so masters were purchased in a range of $200,000 to $500,000. Mellon's eye was getting better, and he drove a hard bargain. In 1928 he purchased his first Raphael for $836,000 (over $16 million in today's dollars), the highest price yet paid for a painting. Works by Hals, Rembrandt, Vermeer, Titian, and Gainsborough followed. Mellon's "coup d'matre" as a collector came with his purchase of twenty-one of the world's greatest paintings from the Hermitage in St.

Petersburg. The Soviets needed money and wanted to make a large deal quietly; Mellon was their man. The bag this time included Hals, Raphael, Van Eyck, Veronese, Rembrandt, and Botticelli. Mellon continued to make major purchases until the year before his death in 1937. His art was no longer a private collection but a national treasure.

During the '20s Mellon was a symbol of all that was right about America. With the advent of the New Deal he was politically crucified as being the cause of all that was wrong with the country. No sooner was Roosevelt in office than he recalled Mellon from Britain; he would gladly have stayed on. The Justice Department then instituted a series of suits against Mellon for fraudulent underpayment of taxes. This extended from 1933 until after his death. The grounds for the aggressive prosecution of these suits were shaky at best. Mellon was put on trial simply for being Mellon. Roosevelt was the guiding hand behind this political theater. The Board of Tax Appeals finally exonerated Mellon in December of 1937, unfortunately three months after his death.

A significant portion of Mellon's remaining years upon returning from Britain in 1933 were spent meticulously crafting the gift of his art collection to the nation he had faithfully served for twelve years. In a letter to Franklin D. Roosevelt, Mellon outlined a proposal for his gift and the creation of the National Gallery to display it. At a specific site on the Mall in Washington, D.C., Mellon would erect at his expense a repository for his collection and future additions to be called the National Gallery. He insisted that the gallery not bear his name; this was a significant act of self-effacement but only in part. By being named the National Gallery and not the Mellon Gallery, other major donors would be encouraged over the years to augment the riches of the gallery far beyond Mellon's seeding gift. Thereby his legacy would be made more powerful and more enduring.

The trustees were to be named by Mellon and their successors selected by his initial board, ensuring in a sense Mellon control beyond the grave. He made plain that his offer was subject to no political compromise; it was take it or leave it, period. At a meeting with Roosevelt the deal was formally struck and soon ratified by the Congress. Returning from a very pleasant meeting with the man who had put him on trial for the excesses of the '20s, Mellon remarked to an associate: "What a wonderfully attractive man the president is." Thus at a stroke Mellon gave witness to Roosevelt's infinite capacity to charm, and no less to his own humanity.

For a man whose talents were remarkably unbalanced, A. W. Mellon's achievements were stunning. As a financier he was second only to J. P. Morgan; as an industrialist he ranks with Carnegie, Ford, and Rockefeller. He gave birth to not one, but five Fortune 500 companies: Gulf Oil, Alcoa, Mellon Bank, Koppers, and Carborundum, plus a score of enterprises, each one of which could be the basis for an enduring family fortune. Next to Alexander Hamilton he was arguably the most distinguished occupant of the Treasury seat. For the decade of the '20s he was the world's financier. His gift of the National Gallery was unprecedented. The Andrew W. Mellon Foundation is now one of the nation's largest, with over $4 billion of assets. Indirectly, through his brother Dick's bequests, billions more have been provided.

Despite all this there was a great and enduring sadness in his life. Where was the road wrongly taken? Was it when he ignored Nora McMullen's prophetic warnings against their marriage? Or was it far earlier when the little boy accepted the Judge's charge to shoulder the burden of his all-consuming dynastic vision?

7

SMILIN' CHARLIE SCHWAB: THE JOYS AND SORROWS OF LIFE ON A LARGE CANVAS

CHRISTMAS SEASON WAS IN FULL FLUSH ON DECEMBER 12, 1900 at the University Club in New York, where the city's financial and industrial elite gathered to honor Charles Michael Schwab, the president of Carnegie Steel. Charlie Schwab, a youthful thirty-eight, had held his position for only three years. The list of attendees included railroaders William Vanderbilt, Chauncey Depew, and E. H. Harriman; bankers James Stillman, August Belmont, and Jacob Schiff; along with H. H. Rogers, president of Standard Oil. And to the right of Schwab, in the seat of honor, his bulbous red nose rivaling that of a famous reindeer, sat the imperious J. P. Morgan. Andrew Carnegie organized the dinner, attended the reception, and then moved on to another engagement. Schwab spoke for a half-hour. The man on his right, fingering an unlit Havana, didn't miss a word.

Charlie Schwab. Courtesy of the Library of Congress

Schwab's talk might have been titled "The Future of the Steel Industry." Its theme was the virtues of industry consolidation. He painted a vision of an industrial behemoth, with volumes sufficient to concentrate huge plants upon a single product—what Harvard Business School professor Wickham Skinner would later term "the focused factory." After the speech Morgan guided Schwab to the privacy of a window seat where the two carried on an animated conversation for another half-hour. Morgan concluded by asking Schwab to

visit his office. In that brief conversation, the world's first billion-dollar corporation, United States Steel, was conceived. With a rapidly accelerated gestation period, the birth of the elephantine infant was announced on March 3, 1901.

Charles Michael Schwab was born in 1862 in the town of Williamsburg, Pennsylvania, fifteen miles east of Altoona. Schwab's German grandfather came to the United States from Baden-Baden in 1830. When young Schwab was twelve, his father Joseph moved the family to Loretto, fifteen miles due west of Altoona where his livery business provided the family a modest living.

Charlie Schwab started to school at age five for a short term of three months. After grade school he attended St. Francis College in Loretto—the equivalent of a high-school curriculum. The schooling was sound but heavily laden with moral precepts of the Franciscan founders, notably poverty, chastity, and obedience. The education took, but the moralizing didn't. In later life Charlie diligently and successfully avoided all three admonitions. He was first in his class, but not through unalloyed intellectual capacity, rather by a combination of a good mind and dogged determination. One of his teachers, Brother Ambrose Laughlin, later reflected on his model student: "In all things Charlie was a boy who never said 'I don't know.' He went on the principle of pretend that you know, and, if you don't, find out mighty quick." Supporting a good mind and innate ambition was a phenomenal memory—names, dates, facts, figures—today we would call it a photographic memory.

A notable fillip to his future success might fall under the heading "Music and the Performing Arts." At age four he began to sing in his grandfather's choir. When he was eight, his mother bought a small parlor organ and paid for Charlie's lessons. In grade school and high school plays or recitations he was always the star. He loved to play the showman and

even the clown. He began working for his father, hauling passengers from the railhead at nearby Cresson; during the trip he would regale them with wit and song, earning the moniker of the "singing cabbie."

At seventeen his head was almost turned from a career in industry and commerce when he fell in love with a young actress; she convinced him a brilliant stage career awaited. Had he been a little less smart and a little less ambitious he might have given it a try. His parents soon intervened, and he was sent off to Pittsburgh in 1879.

As a rich and famous man years later, he told of the siren call of the steel industry: "Often I lay on a hillside watching those tongues of flame shoot up in a pall around Johnstown. A boy had before him a place of vague forms, great labors and dancing fires." There was a slight problem with this story. Johnstown lay eighteen miles to the west of Loretto, separated by several high hills. He couldn't have seen a thing, but the truth here is beside the point. Charlie Schwab imagined the red flames and the vast world beyond and that was truth enough.

Regardless of the precise provenance, the great world beyond beckoned, and, in July of 1879, through a family connection, he landed a clerk's job at McDevitt's store in Braddock, near the entrance to Andrew Carnegie's bustling Edgar Thompson Works. Clerking and bookkeeping offered little challenge to Schwab's supple mind. McDevitt was about to show him the door when fortune intervened in the form of Captain Bill Jones, the foremost steel operator in America.

Born in 1839 of Scottish ancestry, Bill Jones was apprenticed at the age of ten as a foundry molder and later machinist. He enlisted in the Union army as a private and rose to command a company, hence "Captain Jones." Alexander Holley, the designer of Edgar Thompson, hired Jones to supervise construction. Carnegie watched Jones at work and

then hired him to run E.T. It was one of the best personnel decisions the canny Scotsman ever made. Charismatic, hard-driving Jones made E.T. the most productive rail mill in the world. Fearless, Jones was about the only man who would talk back to Carnegie. His immediate response to a rebuke from the little Scotsman was a letter of resignation. Like an American Express card, he never left home without a copy. Captain Bill Jones was the king of Braddock.

It turned out that the king bought his cigars at McDevitt's store. The commercial transaction was invariably accompanied by spirited conversation with the quick-witted Schwab who invariably threw in a few quips and an occasional joke. Jones liked what he saw and offered Schwab a job as a surveyor in the E.T. engineering corps. He began work on September 12, 1879. Their friendship was further cemented when it turned out that Jones shared Schwab's love of music. He would later perform at Jones's house and gave music lessons to his children.

With laser-like focus Schwab plotted his course of advancement at E.T. He had a sponsor—the very best. He determined to make himself "indispensible" to his direct supervisors, and ultimately to Bill Jones, in everything he did. His views and modest education left him generally unqualified for every new assignment he received. The technical knowledge he lacked was gained through books and a small laboratory he set up in his home to master steel metallurgy. Naturally on occasion he stumbled, but invariably his more experienced associates and superiors were always willing to give a little boost to Smilin' Charlie; they couldn't help liking the guy.

In addition to promotions at E.T., Jones rewarded Schwab by making him his messenger to Andrew Carnegie. On one occasion when Carnegie was delayed, Schwab seated himself at the piano in Carnegie's parlor and began to play.

When Carnegie came in he stopped, but Carnegie urged him on. He loved music, particularly Scottish tunes and ballads. He asked if Schwab could play his favorites at a party three days hence. Schwab had no Scottish repertoire, but in typical makeshift fashion he rehearsed the selected numbers and performed to Carnegie's delight. Carnegie later complimented Bill Jones on his excellent selection of a messenger. On the slippery climb up the corporate pole you've got to perform, but your performance also has to be visible. Charlie Schwab was now under the eyes of the big guy.

In 1880 Charlie met his future wife, Emma Eurania Dinkey (called Rana by everyone). He lived at the Dinkey boarding house in Braddock. The Dinkeys were originally from Alsace-Lorraine. After three years of courtship they were married May 1, 1883. Rana was two years older than Schwab, and throughout their fifty-five years of marriage they referred to each other as "old lady and lad." The marriage was childless.

Schwab's rise at E.T. was meteoric. In 1886, at the tender age of twenty-four, he was Bill Jones's right-hand man. He was ready for a greater challenge. On Jones's strong recommendation, Carnegie named Schwab general superintendent of the Carnegie Phipps Homestead Works. Homestead was a failed rail competitor to E.T.; Carnegie picked it up for a song. He put in open-hearth furnaces and a structural plant to serve the burgeoning market for steel-frame structures. Schwab's new salary was $10,000 a year ($200,000 in today's money), a nice step up from his $20 per month starting salary six years earlier.

Schwab turned the lagging Homestead plant around. Carnegie was thrilled to have the two most capable steel men in America running the two major units of his empire. But this felicitous state of affairs came to an abrupt halt in September of 1889 when Bill Jones was killed in an explosion at E.T. He was given the equivalent of a state funeral;

ten thousand Carnegie employees and their families lined the street of Braddock to view the funeral procession. Soon after, Schwab petitioned Carnegie for the top job at Edgar Thompson. Carnegie was reluctant to have Schwab leave Homestead but even more reluctant to turn him down: "If you want to have the honor of succeeding to Captain Jones's position I will oblige you." At twenty-seven, Charlie Schwab was the general superintendent of the largest steel works in America. His future appeared limitless.

July 1, 1992 marked the onset of the Homestead strike. Doubtless the most famous strike in U.S. industrial history, it wasn't so much a strike as a lockout. Carnegie and Frick were determined to break the Amalgamated Union they inherited with the purchase of Homestead—and break it they did. At Carnegie's insistence Schwab was sent back over to Homestead as general superintendent in October. He lived in the plant, visiting every nook and cranny many times on a twenty-four-hour-a-day basis. He not only brought the men around but totally reorganized production. By 1900 he had made Homestead the largest steel plant in the world, surpassing E.T. as Carnegie's crown jewel.

But not all was an upward trajectory. His career almost ran up on the rocks over the great armor plate scandal. Some Homestead employees (today's whistle blowers) reported (for a share of the fine) defective plates shipped to the United States Navy. They claimed that the Navy inspectors were duped by a cover-up of defects—probably true. In congressional testimony, Schwab admitted to the charge but defended his actions, charging the Navy inspectors with gross incompetence—also probably true. There had to be a fall guy and clearly Schwab was it. Carnegie, Frick, and Schwab were all pilloried in the press. But in naval parlance Carnegie was a battleship and Frick a heavy cruiser—both too big to sink. Schwab, on the other hand, was a lowly destroyer; he was vulnerable. To their

credit Carnegie and Frick stood by Schwab, but throughout the rest of his career, when controversy surrounded him as it often did, the armor scandal was invariably brought up with a cry like "remember the Maine."

During his rise to the top Carnegie was Schwab's all-powerful sponsor. He had to please Carnegie, as well as navigate the treacherous waters between the founder and the icy strong-willed architect of Carnegie's success—Henry Clay Frick. From the death of Tom Carnegie in 1886 until Frick's final resignation in 1897, both as CEO and non-executive chairman, Frick's stamp of approval on Schwab's activities was decisive.

Schwab's path to the presidency of Carnegie Steel first opened when Frick resigned in 1894 over Carnegie's unwarranted interference in the affairs of the H. C. Frick Coke Company. His replacement, Vice Chairman John G. A. Leishman, was totally dominated by Frick, who upon the intervention of Henry Phipps had come back as non-executive chairman. Leishman was not up to the job, and Carnegie fired him in 1897. Then Carnegie and Schwab did a little dance. Carnegie first offered Schwab a job as vice president of Carnegie Steel. Schwab turned him down: "I am no good at carrying out another man's orders. . . . As superintendent I am boss of all the plants I manage." It was a calculated gamble. Schwab scouted out his potential competition and knew there was nobody else remotely up to the job, save for Frick, and that china lay broken on the floor. On April 12, 1897, he was named president and CEO of the largest and most profitable steel company in America. Along with power came the prospects of vast wealth. His original 1892 partnership stake of 1/3 percent was increased to 1 percent, with a promise of an additional 1 percent after six months on the job. Inside of six months Carnegie wrote Frick: "I vote for giving Schwab 2 percent [more] instead of 1 percent promised. The cheapest man we have at 3 percent." Frick concurred.

Carnegie Steel was a low-cost producer and was run as such. The variable element in labor cost was not headcount, as with a unionized workforce; in nonunion Carnegie mills, headcount was maintained while wages were cut. When Carnegie Steel was undercut by a competitor's lower prices, wages were reduced and prices were cut until the aggressor cried uncle. Prices were then increased, and wages were restored to their original price level. The second element of the company's leadership involved high rates of reinvestment. When new technology promised increased efficiency, the old equipment was torn out and newer machines put in. The philosophy was Carnegie's, but Schwab executed it flawlessly. Frick occasionally held Schwab at bay on the capital front but generally went along. Schwab never had it all his own way. He once proposed, with support from Frick, that they put a rail mill in Chicago. Carnegie said no.

In 1889 Carnegie had made it known that under the right circumstances he would sell out. Frick and Phipps agreed to act as agents for a syndicate to purchase Carnegie's interests. The deal could not be financed and ended badly. Carnegie turned his wrath exclusively on Frick; Schwab was caught in the middle. With Carnegie's ownership of 55.33 percent the outcome was never in doubt. But Schwab had to be careful. Although they got along well and Frick had been a strong supporter, Schwab was never close to Frick: "No man on earth could get close to him or fathom him. He seemed more like a machine, without emotions or impulses." To the relief of all, Frick resigned on December 5, 1899. Frick Coke and Carnegie Steel were then merged into a new entity. The Carnegie Steel Company was capitalized at $420 million. Schwab was thirty-eight, and his stake in the newly merged company was 6 percent, or $19.2 million ($400 million in today's dollars). The bulk of his career lay ahead of him, but in one

sense this was the peak of his life. The sorrows would gradually begin to outnumber the joys.

The four-year run-up from Schwab's assumption of the Carnegie presidency in 1897 until the creation of U.S. Steel in 1901 witnessed profound changes in the steel industry. With the exception of rails and structural shapes, most of Carnegie's raw steel output was sold semifinished to fabricators of nails, wire, tube, and other finished products.

Squeezed by Carnegie on their raw steel, these companies made plans to integrate backward into steel production. Andrew Carnegie's response was immediate and visceral; he would integrate forward into finished products. He ordered Schwab to design a series of ultramodern facilities to dominate the industry and crush the competition. This gave J. P. Morgan, the apostle of orderly markets, instant dyspepsia; Carnegie had to be stopped.

Soon after the famous Christmas dinner, Morgan and his partners huddled with Schwab in the Morgan library. He told Schwab his goal was not to buy out Carnegie but to prevent him from expanding. Schwab quickly disabused Morgan of this idea, telling him that unless Carnegie retired he *would* expand. Morgan closed the meeting by asking Schwab to prepare a list of companies to be included in the new combine; nobody was better qualified to do it. At their next late-night meeting, Morgan reviewed Schwab's list and told him that, if he could get a price from Carnegie, he would do the deal.

Schwab was again in the hot seat. How to do it? Wisely he sought out Carnegie's wife Louise. She was eager for her husband's retirement and became a welcome ally. After a game of golf and a cozy dinner lubricated by a little scotch, Carnegie named a figure—$400 million. Morgan accepted. A few days later Carnegie had second thoughts and told Schwab he didn't want to do it. The younger man looked his slippery

master in the eye and told him he couldn't renege; Carnegie grumbled and then backed down.

With the deal done two of the three parties heaved a sigh of relief: Morgan because he had the unpredictable and potentially destructive Carnegie off the playing field, and Schwab because he was out from under the eye and command of his longtime benefactor. Schwab did not smoke and used alcohol sparingly, but he did like to gamble. His favorite pastime was a Saturday night poker game, and on every trip to Europe since 1886 he managed to hit the tables at Monte Carlo. All this was kept hidden from Carnegie. A far more serious Schwab transgression was an affair with a beautiful, redheaded nurse who was attending to Schwab's sister-in-law at their home. The young lady gave birth to an illegitimate daughter—Schwab's only child. Schwab provided handsomely for her upkeep and saw her faithfully once or twice a year. Until he reached the safe zone of U.S. Steel, Schwab lived in mortal fear of Carnegie's unearthing his secret; Carnegie would have fired him in an instant. His wife did find out and forgave him, but he continued to have a roving eye.

Schwab's three years as the president of U.S. Steel were not happy ones. The root cause was the organization of that sprawling giant (with 213 mills and 78 blast furnaces) into a holding company. As president of Carnegie Steel, Schwab ran the company with only the occasional interference of the majority owner. At U.S. Steel the board impinged significantly on the management prerogatives of the president through the instruments of two powerful committees: executive and finance.

An additional significant impediment to Schwab's freedom of action was the philosophy of the corporation. Carnegie Steel was a growing enterprise, and as a low-cost producer it wielded its cost advantage to carve out an increasing market share. United States Steel at its inception controlled roughly 50 percent of the American steel market. It

was run for stable profits, not growth. The embodiment of this policy was Judge Elbert H. Gary, former president of the Federal Steel Company, the second largest of the merged entities creating U.S. Steel. Gary didn't drink, smoke, gamble, or tell off-colored jokes. Sober as a "judge," we might call him the "anti-Schwab." As chairman of the executive committee he steadily reduced the scope of Schwab's job until it was patently subordinate to his own.

If all this was not enough, Schwab hastened the day of his departure by conduct unbecoming the president of the world's first billion-dollar corporation. As president of Carnegie Steel, Schwab was relatively anonymous. As president of U.S. Steel, the public hung on his every word. Schwab basked in the public eye, but he did not choose his words wisely. In today's parlance he was politically incorrect. He said college was not necessary for success in business, and unions were in all instances inimical to economic growth. In an outspoken, colorful, Smilin' Charlie Schwab the press found an easy target; they never let up. The coup de grace came with their coverage of his 1902 visit to Monte Carlo; the reports were lurid. Headlines of the New York Sun sang out "Schwab Breaks the Bank." Carnegie was livid, and this hurt Schwab to the quick. Morgan defended him but the die was cast, and, after a lengthy leave of absence, Schwab resigned the presidency in August of 1903.

Energetic is a word that easily attaches itself to Charlie Schwab. With his Carnegie wealth at last unlocked, Schwab immediately set about spending it. His mansion, Riverside, at 72nd and the Hudson River was the last and largest of New York's block-long mansions—costing over $5 million ($100 million in today's dollars). It dwarfed those of Frick and Carnegie. It had ninety rooms, six elevators, and its own power plant, which burned ten tons of coal a day. Smilin' Charlie's carbon footprint was not small.

Joseph Boyer, a gifted Canadian inventor/machinist, approached Schwab for venture backing for two inventions: a pneumatic hammer and an adding machine. Schwab backed the hammer (more industrial) and turned down the adding machine. His $100,000 investment reaped a solid return as the Chicago Pneumatic Tool Company. Unfortunately he let the big one get away. The adding machine was backed by Detroit businessman William S. Burroughs. As a manufacturer of computers, the Burroughs Corporation at its peak had a market capitalization well in excess of U.S. Steel.

Then, eight weeks after assuming the presidency of U.S. Steel, as a personal investment, Schwab bought the Bethlehem Steel Company. He was actively involved in the mergers that created American Steel Foundries and the International Nickel Company.

For once his plate seemed a little full. He sold Bethlehem back to the Morgan interests. A year later he bought it back and immediately sold it for a handsome profit to the jerry-built U.S. Shipbuilding Company. In doing so he bought himself a belly full of trouble. U.S. Shipbuilding went into a very messy and well-publicized receivership. Schwab lost money on the U.S. Shipbuilding transaction but remained in control of Bethlehem Steel along with several shipyards. He was not guilty of fraud but that cut no ice with the press: "Schwab Guilty of Big Fraud," "Schwab a Wrecker," "Death Grip of Schwab." They nailed Charlie's hide to the barn door in bleeding strips.

F. Scott Fitzgerald famously proclaimed: "There are no second acts in American lives." With his transformation of Bethlehem Steel, Schwab was to prove him wrong. Bethlehem traced its origins to the Sauconia Iron Company established in 1857. In 1873, under the name Bethlehem Iron Company, it began the production of Bessemer rails. In 1885 it shifted its mix to concentrate on plates and heavy forgings for guns

and engine shafts, becoming the principal supplier to the expanding Blue Water Fleet of the U.S. Navy. When Schwab took over active command of Bethlehem in 1904 it was a relatively small but well run and profitable enterprise.

In typical style Schwab began his reign with a ringing proclamation: "I intend to make Bethlehem the prize steel works, not only in the United States but in the entire world." He moved quickly to diversify the customer base away from the U.S. government. He reduced shipbuilding facilities from seven to three and began production of special steel alloys, large machined pumps and hydraulic presses, and most notably open-hearth steel rails. Convinced he could not run Bethlehem Steel from New York, Schwab closed Riverside and moved to a comparatively modest fifteen-room home in Bethlehem, Pennsylvania.

Frederic W. Taylor, the father of industrial engineering and so-called scientific management, put his initial "time and motion studies" into practice at Bethlehem five years before Schwab's arrival. As one might imagine, scientific management with lots of charts and figures gave Smilin' Charlie a headache. "Slide rule men," as he called them, were soon gone. Rather Schwab gave the departmental superintendents unbridled authority to hit the numbers any way they chose. Industrial engineering would eventually slip into Bethlehem by the backdoor, but Schwab's inspired leadership got the job done early on.

How did tiny Bethlehem Steel grow to become, at the time of Schwab's death in 1939, the second largest steel company in the United States with 60 percent of the capacity of industry leader U.S. Steel? The answer is simple. It was Schwab's discovery, and elevation to CEO, of Eugene Gifford Grace. While the Grace name has gradually been lost in the fog of time, it clearly belongs to the quintet of American steel luminaries, along with Carnegie, Frick,

Schwab, and Ken Iverson, the Nucor CEO and father of the mini-mill.

Grace, fourteen years younger than Schwab, was born in 1876. He graduated from Lehigh University in 1899. A fine athlete, he nearly became a professional baseball player but instead joined Bethlehem. In 1906 Schwab sent him down to Cuba to straighten out the Juragua Iron Mines, Bethlehem's principal iron ore source. He succeeded admirably and returned as general superintendent of the Bethlehem plant. He was named president in 1913 at the age of thirty-seven. Grace was effectively the CEO and remained in that position until a series of strokes forced his retirement in 1957. In a forty-four-year run, Eugene Grace, for both better and worse, stamped his character on Bethlehem Steel in a manner unparalleled in American industrial history. It was a role reversal for Schwab. With Carnegie he ran the company while Carnegie owned it. With Bethlehem he owned it (at least early on) while Grace ran it.

Charlie Schwab always had a quick eye for the main chance. A rare opportunity presented itself to Schwab in the form of an Englishman, Henry Grey, the inventor of a new structural beam. Familiar with structural steel products from his time in Homestead, Schwab boldly introduced the product at Bethlehem as part of his effort to wean the company off government contracts. In cross section, a structural beam looked like the letter "I"—hence "I beams." Until the advent of the Grey beam, structural sections were fabricated by riveting together three plates, with the web for the vertical section and two flanges for the top and bottom. Grey's breakthrough was to produce the I section from a single steel billet by means of a series of complex shaped rolls. The resulting Grey beam eliminated all the fabricating labor and manufacturing; furthermore it provided greater carrying capacity per ton of steel.

But before this revolutionary advance could be marketed it had to be produced, and this required a huge capital outlay of $4.5 million. In 1905 Schwab set out to raise the money. Buffeted by the financial panic of 1907 it was a daunting task. As was his wont, Schwab attacked on all fronts. He sought and received vendor financing. He personally guaranteed several loans and even received money from Andrew Carnegie, signaling a healing in their previous breach. Carnegie paid tribute to Schwab in congressional testimony: "There is not a girder made in America that does not charge the customer for 15 percent of the steel in the beam which is useless. . . . Mr. Schwab is a genius. I have never met his equal." The Grey beam was a thumping success, and fabricated girders soon went the way of the buggy whip.

U.S. Steel was born in a multiplicity of mergers, like a cosmic big bang. Bethlehem grew to become the industry's number-two producer by a series of acquisitions from 1916 to 1922. In 1916 Schwab acquired the Pennsylvania Steel Company with works near Harrisburg, Pennsylvania and a deep water plant at Sparrows Point, Maryland. The latter facility grew under Grace's tenure to become the largest steel plant in the United States. In a whirlwind of activity in 1922 Bethlehem acquired the Lackawanna Steel Company near Buffalo, giving it access to Midwest markets. Six months later it acquired the Midvale-Cambria Steel Company with its principal works in Johnstown, Pennsylvania. With the 1922 acquisitions Bethlehem's footprint was finally established.

Sixty days after the guns of August signaled the outbreak of the First World War, Schwab was called to London by the British government. He huddled with the triumvirate of British war lords: Secretary of War Herbert Kitchener (Kitchener of Khartoum), First Sea Lord John "Jackie" Fisher, and First Lord of the Admiralty Winston Churchill. He left with an order valued at $135 million for a variety of guns

along with a shell order calling for fifty thousand units a day. Soon after came an order for twenty submarines for the Bethlehem shipyards. So valuable was Bethlehem Steel's armaments capacity that first the Germans and later the British tried to buy the company. In 1916 Bethlehem's profits were $61 million, exceeding the total sales of the company from 1904 to 1912. In 1918, the war's final year, President Woodrow Wilson appointed Schwab director general of the Emergency Fleet Corporation. In this capacity he directed the entire U.S. shipbuilding effort.

In 1918 Charlie Schwab was a relatively young fifty-six. He would live another twenty-one years until 1939, but he was at the apogee of his career and of his personal wealth. From here on it was all downhill—not a black diamond, but a gradual and often pleasant green slope.

During the war Schwab began to accumulate land near his boyhood home in Loretto. On his one-thousand-acre plot he built an estate, Immergrun, comprising eighteen buildings with a forty-room main house. Here even the chickens lived in the lap of luxury, with replicas of French cottages replacing traditional chicken coops. He built a nine-hole golf course with every hole a dogleg right. Smilin' Charlie had a problem with his slice, and, if you had his dough, why adjust your swing to the course when you could fit the course to your swing? Immergrun was completed in 1919, just weeks before Carnegie's death. As legend had it the old man asked his secretary to bring him a photograph of Schwab. He looked at it and then closed his eyes for the last time. A true story? Don't bet against it.

During the 1920s and 1930s Schwab was a roving ambassador for Bethlehem Steel. He gave a lot of speeches; they often began like this: "Now, boys, here is a speech written for me by Ivy Lee and Gene Grace filled with the things 'they' think I ought to say. Here is what I think of that idea." Whereupon he

would tear the speech into little bits and toss it at the audience like confetti. And here was the scam. With his photographic memory Schwab glanced at the speech for a few minutes beforehand and then gave it almost word for word.

In 1927 he succeeded Judge Gary as the head of the American Iron and Steel Institute and served until 1934. He remained chairman of Bethlehem Steel at a munificent salary of $250,000 per annum until his death in 1939. He needed the money. It was by no means payment for services rendered but rather a reward for labors long past.

Schwab died bankrupt in 1939. Rana predeceased him by nine months. No details are available, but we can glimpse the outlines of his financial fall. Charlie was always a big spender. And even in the depression-bitten 1930s he economized only moderately. He loved to gamble, but he no more had a gambling problem than he had a drinking problem. The inimical effect of his gambling proclivities showed up in his business practices. He always played the market; he even had a stock ticker installed at Loretto. Doubtless the biggest part of his fortune went with the deluge of 1929. But even in the 1930s he took many flyers on unwise private investments.

As the stories of Carnegie, Frick, and Schwab are closely interwoven in the history of Carnegie Steel and the birth of United States Steel, some metrics might be illustrative. Intelligence: Carnegie in a walk away, then Frick and Schwab. Entrepreneurial skills: again, first Carnegie, Schwab second, and then Frick. Business acumen: Carnegie and Frick head to head, with Schwab way back. Managerial competence: Frick by a nose, then Schwab, Carnegie last. Personality and salesmanship: here it's Schwab hands down, Carnegie a respectable second, and Frick last. In this win, place, and show there is nothing wrong with third place. In golf it would be like comparing Tiger Woods, Jack Nicklaus, Ben Hogan—all world class.

In 1889 Carnegie set forth his philanthropic ideas in a *North American Review* article entitled "Wealth"—later "The Gospel of Wealth." In a nutshell, Carnegie said to give it away. "He who dies rich dies disgraced." Charlie Schwab had a little different take on things: "I disagreed with Carnegie's idea on the best way to distribute his wealth. I spent mine. Spending creates more wealth for everybody." We have no reason to doubt this was said with a straight face and with childlike innocence.

.

8

MICHAEL LATE BENEDUM: A CHARACTER PORTRAIT IN OIL

PITTSBURGH AND STEEL ARE VIRTUALLY SYNONYMOUS. Less well known is Pittsburgh's rich heritage in the oil business. In 1854 inventor and businessman Samuel L. Keir built the nation's first oil refinery as a crude five-barrel still, one hundred feet away from today's U.S. Steel Building. In 1859 Colonel Edwin L. Drake drilled the first oil well and struck oil at fifty-nine feet in Titusville, Pennsylvania. Drake's successful well opened the Western Pennsylvania oil fields, setting the stage for the auto industrial age. The economy of the twentieth century would surge forward on a sea of oil. Andrew Carnegie made his first big money speculating in oil. In 1874 Charles Lockhart sold Pittsburgh's largest refinery, Lockhart & Frew, to Standard Oil for stock. He rode the ballooning fortunes of Standard to amass a considerable fortune.

And of course the Mellon fortune, Pittsburgh's greatest, rested in large measure on oil. In 1901 A. B. and R. W. Mellon

backed Anthony Lucas, the Austrian prospector who brought in Spindletop, a spectacular 100,000-barrel-a-day gusher near Beaumont, Texas. Thus the first big Texas oilmen were not Texans, but Pennsylvanians. Their nephew W. L. Mellon went on to build the Gulf Oil Corporation into one of the seven sister international oil companies fast in the ranks of Standard of New Jersey, Texaco, and Shell.

Here is a quick primer on the oil business. It may be divided into upstream and downstream activities. Upstream activities involve exploration and production. Exploratory wells are drilled where no oil has been previously found. This is frequently referred to as wildcatting. Once oil is discovered, additional development wells are drilled to prove out the field. Downstream activities involve pipelines and refineries, along with retail and industrial sales. An integrated oil company covers the entire range of upstream and downstream operations.

The preeminent figure in Pittsburgh oil history is Michael Late Benedum (1869–1959). Mike Benedum is universally known as the "king of the wildcatters." He found more oil in more places in the world than anyone in the history of the oil business. This is his story.

Mike Benedum was born in 1869 in Bridgeport, West Virginia. Bridgeport lies in northern West Virginia, one hundred miles due south of Pittsburgh. His parents, Emanuel Benedum and Caroline Lantz Benedum, were of German and English extraction. Mike was the next to last born in a family of six. His mother named him after their beloved family physician Michael Late. Even before Mike's birth, Emanuel had settled on his career. Emanuel Benedum was a close friend of Thomas J. "Stonewall" Jackson, the redoubtable Civil War general who wrote legend in the Shenandoah Valley. As a prosperous landowner and merchant, Emanuel could afford the necessary preparatory education for West Point. However,

Michael Late Benedum. Courtesy of the Library of Congress

when his father's financial prospects faded, Mike began to work to support his family. He quit school at age sixteen after ten years of four months' schooling per year.

Mike's first job at the Davison Flour Mill in Bridgeport paid him $16 a month for a twelve-hour day. He worked at the Davison mill for two years, learning a broad array of skills. His meager salary remained unchanged. He left for a competing mill as manager at $35 a week and soon after took a third position at $50 a week. He probably spent no more than $10 a month on himself, with the remaining money going to his parents and into a modest savings account. From the very

inception of his career, young Benedum was a sedulous accu-
mulator of capital.

Benedum's four-year career as a mill manager ended
tragically when his coat sleeve was caught in the massive gears
of a grinding mill. The badly mangled arm was saved, but his
days in mill work were over. He soon secured a sales job for a
line of mill equipment. He knew the market and the pay was
a bounteous $100 a month. Most important, he learned he
could sell. In later years he exercised these sales skills at the
highest level. Still unsatisfied he quit the job and determined
to seek opportunity in the bustling river town of Parkersburg,
West Virginia, seventy-five miles west. He boarded the train
but never made it to Parkersburg.

Seated in the B&O smoking car on the way to
Parkersburg, young Benedum observed an older man search-
ing for a seat. He graciously offered the man his seat and
insisted that he take it. They then began a conversation that
set Mike Benedum's life on a new course. The stranger was
John Worthington, the general superintendent of the South
Penn Oil Company, a unit of the gargantuan Standard Oil
Company. South Penn ran all of Standard's operations in
West Virginia. Worthington was immediately impressed by
the tall, blue-eyed, straight-backed young man. He offered
him a job with the South Penn. "Well," said Benedum, "I'm
looking for a job. What's the future in it?" A soft smile broke
over Worthington's face. "Oh yes, there's a future." Benedum:
"Thank you sir, I'll do it." This was the start of a seventy-year
run in the oil business for Michael Late Benedum.

Worthington first assigned young Benedum to lease
targeted property for future drilling. He was given $500 in
twenties and fifties and a list of names. One name on the list
was a prominent farmer who had been a consistent holdout.
This happened frequently in the leasing business, and such
target names were called "king bees." The new leasing agent

introduced a few new wrinkles into his lease solicitation as he set out to see the "king bee." He first stopped at a bank and turned in his large bills for all singles. He reasoned that, as he counted out the dollars, a stack would be much more impressive than a few larger denominations. When he met the farmer he politely suggested that his wife might join in the conversation, which started with farming and then segued into oil. The farmer's wife knew exactly what she could do with the mounting stack of one-dollar bills. After the farmer agreed to sign, Mike capped the proceedings with a third and final gambit by engaging the farmer for a fee of $10 a day to accompany him to see his friends and neighbors on the rest of the list.

When Mike reported back the next day, his bosses asked if he had made any dent in the list. The leasing veterans did not have overly high expectations of their young rookie. They thought it might be a little bit like selling encyclopedias, with the hits few and far between. In his quiet but confident manner Mike replied that he believed he had leases from all the names on his list. Mike placed the leases on the table, along with a large stack of bills; he had only used half of his allotted money. When John Worthington was apprised of the results, twenty-year-old Michael Benedum had a loyal and powerful supporter; he was on his way.

Worthington always referred to Mike as "my son." It was almost a filial relationship. Still, Mike soon asserted his independence. Worthington sought a tract of 1200 acres in Monongahela County that was a "must have" for South Penn. He authorized Mike to go as high as one dollar an acre. The owner of the 1200 acres fixed Mike right in the eye and said he was a "one price man." There would be no bargaining. Did Mike understand? He did. The price was ten cents per acre. Mike said he would have to go call the office in Mannington to get approval. Worthington was overjoyed: "See if you can

get it for five cents an acre." Mike exploded. "I'll be damned if I do," he said and slammed down the receiver. He went back and closed the deal for ten cents an acre. This incident only heightened Worthington's respect for Mike, and he recounted the story endlessly.

In 1894 Mike's stellar performance at South Penn was rewarded when John Worthington appointed him assistant general land agent at a salary of $150 per month. He moved to Cameron, West Virginia in the northern panhandle where he had responsibility for all of South Penn's operations in Marshall County, West Virginia and Green County, Pennsylvania.

In the early days of the oil industry, leases were often disputed and occasionally property was leased more than once. Some disputes went to court while others were settled on the spot with the threat of violence and sometimes raw force. Shortly after taking his new position Mike was faced with a Pittsburgh promoter who strong-armed a South Penn crew operating on a bona fide lease. Taking along a couple of burly roughnecks, Mike rode out to the property on horseback. He faced a group of ten armed men. Mike dismounted and walked toward the oncoming trouble. Seconds before violence erupted, their leader, a giant of a man yelled "Stop! It's my friend, Mike Benedum." Two weeks earlier Mike had made the man a small loan. He explained the situation and agreed to pay the invading crew more than their Pittsburgh employer; the big man walked away happy. Mike then hired two hundred men to guard the property until the South Penn wells came in.

Despite his success, Mike was ready to strike out on his own. With his more conservative brother, Charlie, Mike had invested in lease royalties. A lease royalty is created when a lease holder sells his future income stream for cash today. Mike's royalty income gave him a taste of the compounding power of capital. It whetted his appetite for independence.

One summer day in 1895, Joseph Clifton Trees, a former engineer at South Penn, spotted Mike having lunch at the Parriott Hotel. He had a proposition to pitch. It was a fateful meeting and the beginning of a remarkable fifty-year partnership. Drilling was about to begin on a very promising farm in Pleasants County, West Virginia. Needing ready cash, the owner was willing to sell 50 percent of his one-eighth interest for $2,000. Joe optioned the property for $2000 and sealed the deal with $45. It was all the money he had after drilling seventeen dry wells in a row. He asked Mike to put up the remaining $1955.

Mike had known Joe Trees at South Penn and held him in high regard. The red-headed Joe Trees was six feet and three inches of solid muscle. He was one of the outstanding football players at the Western University of Pennsylvania, later the University of Pittsburgh. In those pre-NCAA days Joe also played professional football, for which he was paid a desperately needed $75 a game. Collegiate schedules were irregular in those days. The University of Pittsburgh scheduled a Saturday game with Penn State on the same day Joe had a pro game. Knowing they could not win without Joe Trees, Pitt convinced Penn State to reschedule the game. Joe got his $75, and Pitt later won the game.

Mike studied the property maps for a few minutes and agreed to back Joe for a three-quarter interest in his royalty. It was a bet on Joe Trees as much as it was on geology. It was the first of a long run of winning bets. How good was it? Mike: "In three or four years it paid me my interest several times over. I sold it to my brother Charlie at a nice profit. Charlie got his money out of it with a good profit and sold it to Joe Trees. It returned Joe's investment three times over and he sold it back to me. I got my money back again and a piece of the royalty continued to bring me small returns for thirty years thereafter."

That summer Mike bought leases on 1500 acres south of Cameron near Fish Creek. He paid a pricey $5 per acre for $7500 in all. With John Worthington on vacation, his immediate supervisor came down from Pittsburgh and accused Mike of taking a kickback on the leases. Not believing his ears, Mike quit on the spot. Convinced that he had caught a thief red-handed, the South Penn executive insisted that Mike personally buy the leases. Dead certain of their value Mike borrowed $7500 and bought the leases from South Penn.

Noah Clark, president of South Penn, rushed down from Pittsburgh in an attempt to save their rising star. Mike didn't change his mind but did agree to help Clark pick up some valuable leases in Green County, Pennsylvania. He paid his own expenses and did not charge Clark for his work. Two days later a gracious letter arrived from Clark, commending Mike for his valuable contribution to South Penn; enclosed was a check for $5000.

In May 1896 Mike married Sarah Lantz, the daughter of a prosperous farmer from whom he had leased oil rights. In Mike's words, the Lantz family was "well informed, friendly, God-fearing—a family like his own." A year later their first and only child was born, a boy, Claude Worthington Benedum, in honor of John Worthington.

Oil leases became more or less valuable depending upon the failure or success of wells drilled in near proximity to the leasehold. In mid-1896 the Fish Creek leases for which Mike had paid $7500 were becoming hot properties as South Penn drilled a succession of producing wells on property bordering Mike's leases. South Penn, in an unwise choice of a negotiator, sent down the man who had forced Mike to buy back the leases. His opening offer was Mike's price of $7500; his final offer was $75,000. The hardnosed Benedum turned them all down.

South Penn now turned up the heat by drilling several wells right on the line, in some cases slanting the drill bore

onto Mike's property, threatening to drain his oil. South Penn's actions were at best unethical and probably illegal. Mike needed to drill several wells on his leases and drill them fast. He had no money. He went to several drillers hat-in-hand, asking them to drill on the come. Several drillers agreed to do this because they believed in the leases, but more importantly because they believed in Mike Benedum. Nineteen wells successfully came in, but Mike still needed to come to terms with South Penn's parent.

John D. Archbold was John D. Rockefeller's right-hand man and the operating head of the Standard Oil behemoth. Archbold was forty-eight; Mike was twenty-seven. His age probably worked in his favor. Through intermediaries, including Archbold's son who had worked with Mike at South Penn, a meeting was arranged with the oil titan in New York. By all odds, Benedum should have been squeezed out by Standard with only modest compensation. By Mike's reckoning his properties were worth $250,000. Until the very last, he insisted on $600,000 and made a strong case for this value. He finally settled for $400,000, or $8 million in today's money. This was the first big-league demonstration of Mike's legendary negotiating skills.

The years from 1897 until the Illinois play in 1905 were lean years for Mike Benedum. By 1902 he had lost the whole $400,000 and was deep in debt. Several factors propelled his fall from the heights to the depths.

In 1901 the Mellon-backed Spindletop blew in near Beaumont, Texas, at the incredible rate of one hundred thousand barrels a day. In short order the price of crude plummeted ten cents a barrel. This put pressure on Mike's royalty payments and made future drilling in West Virginia far less profitable than before. Before the turn of the century the primary sources upon which the Standard was built rested in a triangle from northwestern Pennsylvania to western Ohio

(Lima), to northern West Virginia. Indeed no less a figure than John D. Archbold, when told about promising signs of oil in Oklahoma, exclaimed: "Are you crazy, man? Why I'll drink every gallon of oil produced west of the Mississippi." In the new century the center of gravity for oil production moved southwest to Oklahoma, Texas, Louisiana, and later to California.

Compounding Mike's problems was his decision at the urging of his older and more conservative brother Charlie to diversify his holdings out of oil into much "safer" banking and manufacturing. He put significant money in the First Citizens Bank and became its chairman. In three years' time his glass and pottery manufacturing companies were bankrupt and First Citizens was forced to close its doors. Of course, when it rains it pours; Mike and Joe Trees also drilled a long string of dry holes.

In 1904 Charlie Benedum died, leaving his widow and an infant son Paul Gregory Benedum. Paul was to have a long and fruitful association with his uncle Mike. At about this time Mike and Joe Trees set up the Benedum Trees Oil Company with offices in Wheeling, West Virginia. Benedum Trees was more of a holding company than an operating company. Each new play stood on its own. If Joe came in with Mike, most often they were fifty-fifty partners. Mike or Joe could come in or opt out as they chose. Mike was invariably in, and on occasion Joe would opt out.

In 1905 they went to Casey, Illinois in the southeastern part of the state at the request of a leaseholder. Prospects did not look good, and Mike Benedum's old mentor John Worthington had been through the territory and offered him fatherly advice: "Don't get burned, my son." About ready to decamp for Wheeling, they came upon a bizarre-looking itinerant dressed in formalwear, claiming to be a geologist. The locals regarded him as a crank. Prevailing wisdom saw

the "trend" (the path of the underlying oil) as going north-east to southwest. The stranger said that in this case the trend ran northwest to southeast, and that they might hit pay dirt in Robinson, Illinois, thirty miles southeast. After thoroughly investigating the Robinson area, they leased up fifty thousand acres on the cheap for ten cents an acre. Nobody thought there was any oil to be found near Robinson. Being short on funds they parceled out 9/20 to Pittsburgh investors and retained 11/20 for Benedum Trees.

The first well came in at twenty-five barrels a day, the second at two thousand. It was a major field. In 1904 Illinois had not been credited with a single barrel of oil production. In 1907 it produced twenty-four million barrels and ranked third nationally. An army of oil prospectors moved in and within weeks sunk wells by the hundreds. Benedum Trees had to drill furiously to protect its reservoir. Joe was the driller and engineer and Mike the financier, trader, and sales-man. Their talents meshed perfectly. They ended up selling, on extended payment terms, to the flamboyant Theodore Barnsdall. When the first payment was due, Barnsdall didn't have the money but sold a piece of the increasingly valuable property. He did the same thing all the way through and never laid out a nickel. Mike and Joe ended up with $2 mil-lion ($40 million in today's money) on the deal.

In 1907 Mike and Joe relocated Benedum Trees from Wheeling to Pittsburgh, feeling they could better operate out of this oil and financial center. On the advice of Ted Barnsdall, they decided to investigate opportunities in Caddo Parish, south of Shreveport, Louisiana. Characteristically, they leased big—130,000 acres. After four shallow wells came up dusters, they decided to try one last deep well; it came in at 3600 barrels a day. It opened up the fabulous Caddo Field, which by the end of 1952 had produced 185 million barrels. One technical problem remained, and Joe Trees solved it.

The soil kept caving in at the borehole. Joe cemented the hole and then drilled through the cement; problem solved.

Finding oil is one thing; selling it is something else. The buyer of last resort was as always the Standard. They offered Benedum Trees thirty-nine cents for oil they resold at $1.40. The Rockefeller behemoth was squeezing the life out of Benedum Trees. Mike Benedum donned his selling cap and set out selling his oil to Standard customers at $.70 a barrel. It was a price he could live with and a bargain for the Standard buyers. Mike then threatened to build a refinery in direct competition with Standard. A call soon came out from Standard to come to its headquarters at 26 Broadway. A deal was going to be made, but what kind of deal? Before Mike and his two partners left for 26 Broadway, Mike had a "come to Jesus" talk with Joe Trees and Harry Grayson. He told Joe he was the best petroleum engineer in the country, but not the best negotiator. Grayson and Trees agreed to let Mike have absolute control of the talks. The three agreed that $3 million was a very acceptable price.

Three of Archbold's chief lieutenants led off with an offer of $2 million. Mike got up and said: "Come on, boys. Let's go back to Pittsburgh." The Standard team excused themselves several times, obviously going down the hall to confer with Archbold. Grayson and Trees were tickled to death when they came back with their target figure of $3 million. Mike responded: "Boys, get your hats." $5 million now came on the table. Grayson and Trees had their tongues hanging out down to their belt buckles. Mike: "Well, boys, if we hurry down to Penn Station, we can catch the 5:00 p.m. train." Mike was close but not quite there. He told the Standard negotiators he was tired of dealing with seconds. He wanted to settle things principal to principal—Benedum and John D. Archbold. The big man himself finally came in and Mike respectfully and persuasively convinced Archbold

that the Caddo concession would yield fifty million barrels. It turned out to be a gross underestimation. The deal closed at $6 million, yielding Mike Benedum over $2 million, or $40 million in today's money. And, as the frosting on the cake, the Benedum investors retained all the gas rights. Oftentimes the best salesmen are not the best negotiators and vice versa. Mike Benedum combined both skills at the highest level and balanced them in delicate equipoise.

By 1911, Michael Benedum and the Benedum Trees Oil Company were well established in Pittsburgh, but the family and the company were still renters. Mike and Sarah Lantz Benedum deepened their ties to Pittsburgh by buying and then tearing down the old Howell mansion on Fifth Avenue at South Highland. On this seven-acre property with eight hundred feet fronting on Fifth Avenue, they built Graystone, one of Pittsburgh's finest mansions. That same year Benedum Trees found a new home at 223 Fourth Avenue in the nineteen-story McChesney Building, then renamed the Benedum Trees Building. Over the next forty years Mike and Joe shared adjoining offices on the fifteenth floor. The building was eventually filled with a layer cake of Benedum companies, including Tropical, Arkansas Natural Gas, Hiawatha, Wayne Coal, Plymouth, and several others. Mike Benedum was the guiding light of all these organizations, but he was never an officer nor did he draw a penny of salary. His wealth came exclusively from his equity ownership.

Mike and Joe Trees moved quickly to exploit their residual natural gas concessions from the Caddo deal with Standard. They began by forming Arkansas Natural Gas Company, always referred to as the "Ark." Backed by their usual coterie of Pittsburgh investors, the Ark was capitalized at $10 million in 1911. Drawing its gas from the Caddo fields, the Ark served residential and industrial users in southeastern Arkansas. The Ark was a troubled company right from

the start. It did manage to lay 485 miles of pipeline into Arkansas but diminished gas supplies and pipeline problems, along with a succession of dry holes, kept profits stubbornly low. In 1918 the bottom line yielded a meager $50,000, and the stock languished at $5 a share. Then the Benedum magic struck. In May 1919, a large wildcat well came in thirty-five miles south of the Caddo in Claiborne Parish, near Homer, Louisiana. Mike told the Ark people to get any leases they could near the strike. They did manage to get an option on 120 acres at the outrageous price of $500 an acre. They told Pittsburgh it was too much to pay. Benedum: "Get it . . . or Joe and I will carry it ourselves."

The Homer well came in at twenty-five thousand barrels a day, with oil selling at a handsome $3.58 a barrel. Ark stock had a nice run-up in the next week; it went from $5 to $400 a share. Within three years the Homer leases yielded $7 million on an investment of $60,000—better than a one thousand to one return. In the late 1920s Mike and Joe sold their holdings to Henry L. Doherty's Cities Service Company.

After two successful plays in Mexico at Tampico and along the Tuxpam River, Mike Benedum was ready to extend his search for oil globally. In 1915 one of his partners from the Mexican foray secured a fabulous three-million-acre concession deep in the jungles of Columbia, 375 miles up the Magdalena River. Mike always thought big; three million acres was certainly big. An on-sight inspection showed oil in the concession was knee-deep in pools. It was almost impossible to bring drilling equipment and men in, and even more difficult to get the oil out. Mike Benedum proved equal to the challenge. From his Pittsburgh partners and the public he raised $50 million to fund the Tropical Oil Company. The field was proved out, and the oil was close to high-quality Pennsylvania crude. But Tropical lacked the money to build a 400–mile pipeline through to the coast.

Fortuitously, a call came in from 26 Broadway. The Standard man said: "How much do you want?" Mike allowed as how he didn't want cash, but would take stock and stay in the game. International Oil, a Standard subsidiary, gave them 25 percent of the company, valued at $32 million. Mike came out of the deal with $7 million, or $140 million in today's dollars. Mike called the Infantas one of the great fields of all time.

No state in the union is more associated with oil and oil money than Texas. Shortly after the turn of the twentieth century it became the largest oil producer in the United States. Four signal events established Texas as the crown jewel of the U.S. oil industry. First came Spindletop in 1901; second, well #9 established the Big Lake field, a small part of the vast Permian Basin extending across West Texas into New Mexico in 1924; third, Yates #1 in 1926; and, lastly, in 1930 "Dad" Joiner's Daisy Bradford #3 opened the vast east Texas oil fields, the largest in U.S. history. Mike Benedum was the only U.S. oil man to bring on two of the four fields: Big Lake/ Permian and Yates.

In May 1923 Frank Pickeral, a hustling World War I veteran and former soda jerk, brought in Santa-Rita number 1 at a hundred barrels a day. It was a well but barely. Pickeral and his Texon Oil Company brought it in on a shoestring, and he needed help. On the advice of several Texas oil men, he went to see Mike Benedum in Pittsburgh. Mike was then suffering from a lengthy string of dry holes and suggested young Pickeral talk to Gulf, Jersey Standard, and others. Three months later, with no takers, he came back with renewed fervor and repitched his case to Benedum. Outstanding salesmen have an Achilles heel. They are often a soft touch for an equally skilled pitchman with a solid story. Mike Benedum was no exception; he was bitten. He excused himself and strode across to Joe Trees's office. Joe: "Don't do it, Mike. If the majors don't want it, you don't want it." It wasn't the

first time Mike ignored Joe Trees's advice. He cut a deal with
Pickeral when the latter had his back to the wall; Frank would
have settled for anything Mike offered. Having been a shoe-
string operator himself, Mike gave him a very fair deal. He
would provide the money for eight wells, leaving Frank a gen-
erous 25 percent.

To pursue the project Mike organized the Plymouth Oil
Company. Turned down by several of his stalwart investors,
Mike syndicated the Plymouth flotation with a number of
wealthy West Virginians. He took 25 percent and, at the last, a
reluctant Joe Trees committed for 5 percent. The eight wells
were either dry holes or very marginal producers; Plymouth
was out of money. Like a poker player shoving in his last
stack, Mike advanced $800,000. Wells nine and eleven proved
the field. Profits were dazzling. In 1926 Plymouth paid divi-
dends of $5.5 million. Unlike Caddo, Columbia, and other
big strikes, Plymouth held onto the stake and moved down-
stream; it became the principal operating company of the
Benedum interests.

The Yates field came in at the end of a notable Benedum
failure—his attempt to build an integrated oil company. In
1919 he combined several disparate Benedum units into the
Transcontinental Oil Company. The stock opened in August
of 1919 at $48 a share. Three years later it was slinking along
at $1.50 a share. With the Transcontinental it was Murphy's
Law—everything that could go wrong did go wrong.

Then Ira Yates walked in the door. Ira had a ranch west
of the Pecos, one hundred miles east of San Angelo, Texas.
He was certain he had oil under his ranch and finally con-
vinced Mike Benedum's field man, Levi Smith, who in turn
sold Mike. The tenth commandment of the Texas oil business
stated flatly: "There is no oil west of the Pecos." It was at least
a hundred to one shot and a bold gamble even for the Great
Wildcatter. Mike hedged his bet by bringing in the Ohio

Company to drill four wells in return for 50 percent. They were not drilled on the Yates ranch but on other Benedum lease holdings close by. All four were dusters. Smith reminded Benedum of his promise to drill the Yates ranch. Mike, true to his word, said if necessary he would do it himself. He finally convinced Ohio Oil to drill the fifth well on Yates's ranch. On October 28, 1926, Yates number 1 came in at four thousand barrels a day. Seventy wells were drilled on the Yates lease. In 1929, 70-A came in at the Golcondic rate of 204,000 barrels a day. Yates was arguably the richest concentrated field in U.S. oil history. Ohio bought out Transcontinental for $60 million. Until his death, Michael L. Benedum remained one of Ohio Oil's largest shareholders. Today the Yates Field has produced over a billion barrels and is still going strong.

Any one of the great Benedum strikes—Caddo, Columbia, Big Lake, Yates, and others—would ensure a man's place among the storied figures of the oil industry. The Benedum story goes far beyond these headlines. Like diamond baguettes clustered around master stones, there are a host of successful yet secondary plays. Mike Benedum wild-catted in Turkey, Romania, Canada, and along the Texas Gulf coast. There were also in his wildcat career of over sixty-five years many failures.

Mike Benedum began to winter at the Rony Plaza Hotel in Miami Beach during the 1920s. Sitting outside his cabana with clerical help and a full complement of phone gear, attired in his normal beach garb—coat, tie, vest, fedora hat, and black wing tips—Mike thought there must be some oil off Miami Beach. The well ran way over on cost and a hurricane blew away much of the gear—no oil, a total loss. He turned back to fishing. There was lots of coal in West Virginia and Pennsylvania. Why not try the coal business? With his Wayne Coal Company he lost millions. The most far-out prospecting he did was for gold—and in, of all places, Virginia. You

already know the outcome. Joe Trees summed it up well: "Money has always been a by-product with Mike. The thrill of discovery has been his only goal."

The most ambitious projects he ever undertook never got off the ground, but they fully demonstrate the power and scope of his fertile imagination. In the 1920s a Peruvian railroad engineer presented Mike and Joe with a claimed lease on sixty-four million acres deep in the Peruvian jungles, bigger than West Virginia and Pennsylvania combined. Mike verified the existence of the oil by sending down prominent Pittsburgh geologist L. G. Huntley. The scope of the project went far beyond the oil. The plan envisioned mass colonization from Germany, Spain, and Italy and perhaps the creation of a new Andean nation. Mussolini alone promised one million Italian immigrants. As usual with Il Duce he promised much and delivered little. Even the cautious Joe Trees liked this deal. It never happened.

Could there possibly be anything bigger than the Andean Empire scheme? As a matter of fact there was: China. Through his intermediaries' discussions with Chiang Kai-Shek and his foreign minister, the slippery T. V. Soong, he was offered the exclusive drilling rights in all of China. Mike wasn't sure about where the oil was in China but, with the whole damn country, there had to be something. It was a reasonable hunch. The Japanese invasion of China in 1937 put the quietus on project China.

Although he slowed down a little bit, Mike remained active in the 1950s. He finally succumbed to old age in 1959 at the age of ninety. He had no survivors. His wife predeceased him, and their only child, Claude Worthington Benedum, fell victim to the influenza epidemic of 1919. Three Benedum nephews worked for the Benedum interests. Paul G. Benedum took over several of Mike's duties during the 1950s.

Mike once said: "If you make much money in the oil business at all you make it very rapidly." Most great fortunes are accumulated over time. The oil business is like a Keystone Kops movie running in fast motion. Its hits and misses are scored instantaneously.

Mike Benedum left an estate of $70 million. Half went to collateral relatives and half funded the Claude Worthington Benedum Foundation. In 2007 its assets were over $400 million. Two-thirds of this goes to Mike's home state of West Virginia. The steady gaze from those blue eyes that first caught the attention of John Worthington in 1890 emanated a strong sense of character. That character enabled Mike Benedum to do the near impossible and do it for over seventy years.

9

SOLDIER/STATESMAN: THE GREATNESS OF GEORGE CATLETT MARSHALL

On September 1, 1939, as German troops thundered across the Polish border, General George C. Marshall succeeded Malin Craig as the U.S. Army Chief of Staff. One week later, Marshall returned to his birthplace and childhood home in Uniontown, Pennsylvania, forty-six miles southeast of Pittsburgh for a homecoming celebration. The man President Harry Truman was to call "the greatest military man this country has ever produced" had deep roots in Western Pennsylvania. His father is buried there in the Allegheny cemetery, and his sister, Marie, spent her adult life in Greensburg. Thus we may rightly and proudly claim George Marshall as a son of the Pittsburgh region.

The last of four children, Marshall was born in 1880. His father, George Sr., was a leading citizen of Uniontown. He made and lost a small fortune in the coke and coal business. A collateral relative was the great chief justice, John Marshall.

George Catlett Marshall. Courtesy of the Library of Congress

Young George was bored with his family genealogy: "Continual harping on the name John Marshall was kind of poor business. It was about time for someone else to swim for the family." And, of course, swim he did.

For reasons not entirely transparent, George Marshall fixed upon a military career. His parents were opposed. George Sr. was a prominent Democrat, and Pennsylvania's two senators, Penrose and Quay, were both Republicans—no senatorial appointment, no West Point. And beyond appointment lay competitive examinations. George Marshall was a poor student; he did get better but he was never outstanding. The Virginia Military Institute (VMI) in Stanton, Virginia

offered a reasonable compromise. His older brother, Stuart, graduated in 1894. VMI was by no means the West Point of the South. It was principally an engineering school, and in 1891 fewer than ten VMI graduates were on duty with the regular army. With some sacrifice the family scraped together the tuition, and George was off to VMI in 1897.

Marshall's four years at VMI clearly stamped him as a military man. At the end of his first year he was named first corporal. Then successively he was named first sergeant and, for his final year, the prestigious first captain. In his words: "What I learned at VMI was self-control [and] discipline so that it was ground in."

A comparison to his age peer Douglas MacArthur (b. 1880) is illustrative. The son of Lieutenant General Arthur MacArthur, governor of the Philippines and vice chief of staff for the U.S. Army, the young MacArthur was both first captain and academically first in his class—the first cadet in West Point's history to attain these twin pinnacles. Destiny was his helpmate and he knew it. More intellectual, far better educated, and better looking (L. B. Mayer would never have chosen a George Marshall lookalike to play the lead in a MacArthur movie), MacArthur certainly held all the cards. In ambition they were equal, but ultimately Marshall's character, integrity, and judgment won the day, but early on you couldn't see it. It was to be a slow forty-year slog.

To secure his coveted commission young Marshall, with the full support of his father, began to lobby hard. Secretary of War Elihu Root and Attorney General Philander C. Knox (a Pittsburgher), along with Pennsylvania senators Quay and Penrose, were courted by the two Marshalls. The capstone of Marshall's efforts was George's attempt to meet with President McKinley. Having no appointment, Marshall walked in the front door of the White House and up the stairs to McKinley's office. The head usher asked him if he had an

appointment and Marshall said "no." Under those circumstances, the usher said, he would not be able to see the president. At that moment a man and his daughter were admitted to see the president, and Marshall simply attached himself to this little procession and walked in. Their business done, the father and daughter left, leaving Marshall standing before the president. He promptly and succinctly stated his case and left. This may or may not have been the turning point, but this action certainly cut him out from the herd. He was commissioned a second lieutenant on February 2, 1901.

He was married the following year to a Lexington girl (Elizabeth Coles) four years older, with social credentials much surpassing his own. He began his career in the Philippines, then moved to Fort Reno, Oklahoma, and from 1906 to 1910 was at the Army Staff College, Fort Leavenworth, Kansas. The work was rigorous and demanding but not intellectually challenging. He graduated first in his class and was promoted to first lieutenant in 1907. During that time he was assigned duty with the Pennsylvania National Guard. This experience and several other assignments to various National Guard units gave him a well-earned reputation for training soldiers and a wide network of powerful supporters, both military and civilian. Following Leavenworth he had assignments in Texas, Massachusetts, Florida, and Arkansas, punctuated by time with the National Guard. In 1913 he was sent back to the Philippines. Despite a brilliant record in each and every posting, along with a growing reputation, at age thirty-five Marshall was still a first lieutenant; time was running out. He wrote the superintendent of VMI, General Nichols, telling the general he was thinking of abandoning his army career. Nichols responded: "I advise you to stick with it." It was good advice.

With the war in Europe things began to move, and Marshall was promoted to captain in 1916. The United States

entered the war in April 1917. After the usual military politicking Marshall was placed on the general staff of the First Division, commanded by General W. L. Sibert. The First Division was slow off the dime, and in October of 1917 the commanding general of the Allied Expeditionary Force (AEF), John J. Pershing, took Sibert and his newly appointed chief of staff to task. It was not pleasant. Marshall, who had been acting chief of staff, came to the defense of his superiors and, in a state of some agitation, gave General Pershing his unsolicited statement of the facts as he knew them. Pershing countered; Marshall countered back. Pershing turned on his heel and left. General Sibert thought Marshall just flushed his career down the drain. Much to the contrary, on subsequent visits Pershing invariably sought out Marshall for his views. In fact, Marshall's courageous and foolish challenge of the AEF commanding general initiated the most important and valuable relationship of his military career. By 1917 he was on Pershing's staff.

Marshall finished the war as chief of the operations division of the First Army. He was a temporary colonel and would wait another eighteen years for his first general's star. He soon slipped back into his permanent rank of captain.

In July of 1921 Pershing was named chief of staff, and once again Marshall was his key aide for the entire four years. Officers in more senior billets on the general staff were rotated in and out of their positions but Marshall remained. More and more Pershing's key directives came across his desk. On several occasions he sat in on meetings between Pershing and President Harding. He made a broad range of high-level contacts, including Herbert Hoover, General Charles G. Dawes, Bernard Baruch, and others.

One vignette from this period illustrates Marshall's unique relationship with Pershing. Determined to overturn a policy of his much-disliked predecessor, General Peyton

March, Pershing sent his position paper to Marshall, who penned his strong disapproval. Back and forth it went for two more drafts, until Pershing attempted to close the matter with a decisive "no" to Marshall's proposal. Marshall retorted: "General, just because you hate the guts of General March . . . you're setting yourself up to do something you damn well know is wrong." Pershing folded: "Well, have it your way." This brief dialogue speaks to the heroic status of both men and takes us very close to the heart of Marshall's greatness. There was no charity in Pershing's final acquiescence. Marshall earned Pershing's unqualified support by his unique ability to strike the keys of power year in and year out with barely a discordant note.

When Pershing finished his four-year term in 1925, Marshall left Washington for a three-year tour of duty in China. In 1928 Marshall was made assistant commandant at the infantry school at Fort Benning, Georgia. Through the infantry school passed many of the leaders of World War II and after, including Omar N. Bradley, J. Lawton Collins, Matthew B. Ridgway, Joseph W. (Vinegar Joe) Stilwell, Walter Bedell Smith, and Courtney Hodges. Students were required to present twenty-minute monographs on broad topics. Concision of exposition was the goal. Complaints were voiced that twenty minutes just wasn't enough time. Marshall then took the floor and covered the Civil War in five minutes. Point made. Previously widowed, at Benning he met his second wife, Katherine. By the end of his five years at Benning, Marshall was highly regarded throughout the army by superiors and subordinates alike.

But for the vagaries of the seniority promotion system, Marshall might easily have had his first star in the early '30s. Such was not to be the case. There is some evidence that Douglas MacArthur, then chief of staff (1930–1935), may have held Marshall back over differences they had in

France. MacArthur lacked the tolerance and forbearance of the equally strong-willed Pershing. We cannot be sure. With Marshall it was not about becoming a brigadier general, but rather about *when* he attained the rank, so as to leave sufficient time to receive the second star and then the brass ring: chief of staff. It seemed everybody from Roosevelt on down wrote letters on Marshall's behalf. Pershing in particular made it a crusade and finally, on October 1, 1936, it happened. Unlike most of his peers, Marshall never lobbied directly for consideration, but he was well aware of and appreciated the efforts of others on his behalf.

It was sometimes said that Marshall was a dark-horse candidate for chief of staff, and that Roosevelt with divine guidance picked him out of the crowd. He was always in strong contention with only one other candidate, General Hugh Drum. In 1938 he was named to the War Plans Division of the General Staff and, finally, as deputy chief of staff. This latter move was forced by the strong-willed Louis Johnson, acting secretary of war. But alas, the deputy position no more led to the chief's office than vice president to the Oval Office.

November 14, 1938 saw the new deputy at a White House meeting with administration heavyweights, including Henry Morgenthau (secretary of the Treasury), Harry Hopkins (WPA administrator), and a dozen others. It was Marshall's debut. On a particular issue Roosevelt did most of the talking. His position was greeted with universal approbation. Nearing the end he turned to Marshall and said: "George, don't you think so?" Marshall shot back: "Mr. President, I don't agree with that at all." With a startled look on his face Roosevelt abruptly adjourned the meeting. Some of the attendees told Marshall they felt sorry that his career had come to such an abrupt end.

As a side note Marshall observed: "I remember he called me George. . . . I wasn't very enthusiastic over his misrepresentation of our intimacy. . . . I don't think he ever did it

again." Shortly thereafter at a private meeting he told the president: "Mr. President, don't call me George." Roosevelt, not Marshall, told the story.

"Don't call me George" gets us to the heart of Marshall's famous reserve, even as he became Roosevelt's most important strategic advisor. Marshall kept the president at a calculated distance. He invariably declined invitations to the White House and to Hyde Park. The first time Marshall visited Roosevelt's birthplace was at his funeral. Marshall allowed that informal conversation with the amiable Roosevelt could be dangerous.

Marshall's relationship with Roosevelt was strengthened rather than weakened by his frankness. Harry Hopkins became his champion, and no one was closer to the president than Harry Hopkins. Marshall waged no public campaign for his position. He had wide support from Secretary of War Harry Hines Woodring, as well as General Pershing. Hugh Drum, commander of the First Army, was the front runner but refused to let his preeminence speak for itself. Marshall's more nuanced approach to his candidacy carried the day. In April he was invited to the White House and the job was his.

Effective as he was, Marshall was no workaholic. He maintained a clear divide between his work as chief of staff and his private life with Mrs. Marshall. He enjoyed movies and in particular Westerns, and his reading was limited to novels and magazines. His favorites: the *Saturday Evening Post* and the *Reader's Digest.* Marshall was not an intellectual. His considerable intellect was aimed at solving practical problems. The theoretical and the academic held little interest. With visitors to his office there was a set routine. Enter and take a seat without being asked and with no greeting. When Marshall raised his head from the papers on his desk, start talking. When Marshall put his head back down, get up and leave. It was his special aura of authority that his subordinates, peers, and superiors best remembered.

It is hard to imagine two more disparate personalities than Marshall, the austere and reserved soldier, and Roosevelt, the affable and aristocratic country squire. Marshall made no attempt to mute his reserve; he put it forward as a shield to ward off Roosevelt's disarming charm. His stiffness was underlined by his refusal to laugh at Roosevelt's jokes, many of which were quite funny. It is doubtful if Roosevelt really liked Marshall, for the same reason that he venerated him. "I never argued with the president," Marshall recalled. "I swallowed the little things so I could go to bat on the big ones." When he hit a rough patch, Harry Hopkins always smoothed the way.

On June 22, 1940 Roosevelt appointed Republican Henry L. Stimson as secretary of war. Stimson, seventy-two, had done it all. He served as secretary of war under Taft, governor of the Philippines under Coolidge, and secretary of state under Hoover. He served every administration from Taft to Truman. They were strong-willed men and occasionally argued, but Marshall had Stimson's complete confidence. Marshall's position was considerably buttressed by Roosevelt's executive order of July 5, 1939, authorizing direct contact between the president and chiefs of staff relating to the making of "strategy, tactics and operation." Stimson fully accepted this diktat.

When Marshall entered the drab munitions building as Army chief of staff he commanded an army of 175,000, the seventeenth largest army in the world. He immediately set about building the army that would, by 1944, number eight and three-quarters of a million men—a fifty-fold increase. However, the country was not at war and was not immediately threatened, and strong isolationist sentiment prevailed. Marshall could move no faster than the president, and the president dared not get too far in front of public opinion. Besides, Roosevelt faced an election in the fall of 1940 for an unprecedented third term.

Marshall needed vast sums of money to place his tiny army on a wartime footing. With Harry Hopkins in the hospital, his chosen helpmate was the secretary of the Treasury and Roosevelt's longtime Duchess County neighbor, Henry Morgenthau, Jr. With the exception of Hopkins nobody was closer to the president than Morgenthau. At a pivotal May 13, 1940 meeting with Roosevelt, Morgenthau made the request for a major jump in funding. Roosevelt said "no." He then asked the president to listen to Marshall—another "no." Whereupon Marshall stood up, his volcanic temper only marginally under control. He launched an impassioned plea; the words just poured out. He concluded: "If you don't do something . . . and do it right away I don't know what's going to happen to this country." Marshall got the money. The ascension of Winston Churchill to British prime minister and the subsequent fall of France strengthened the president's hand. In appearing before the Congress Marshall was invaluable. His credibility and character resonated with the lawmakers far better than did the president—often a polarizing figure. In the words of House Speaker Sam Rayburn: "He has the presence of a great man."

Not only did Marshall need a bigger army, he needed to install a vigorous young officer to lead it. He ruthlessly chopped the dead wood out of the static peacetime officers' corps. To reinforce the necessity of this action he twice submitted his own resignation to Roosevelt. The president laughed him off.

Another Marshall fan was Senator Harry S. Truman. Truman built his national reputation and paved his way to the vice presidential nomination in 1944 by leading the "Truman committee," charged with the investigation of top war contracts. From the beginning Marshall bent over backwards to cooperate with Truman and his committee. They developed a healthy mutual respect, which bore great fruit during the Truman presidency.

During the twenty-seven months before Pearl Harbor, Marshall's accomplishments were solid, but only a modest fraction of what was to follow. He put the U.S. Army on a wartime footing. But more important was the foundation he laid for his reputation and influence. Relatively unknown outside of the army in 1939, he now won widespread respect and even deference from the Congress, the administration, and the general public, and, not least, he won and never lost the complete confidence of the ringmaster himself: FDR. He was now ready for the world stage.

Within two weeks of Pearl Harbor, Churchill and a massive British entourage settled in Washington for three weeks of the Arcadia Conference—the first of nine such conferences held throughout the war. Arcadia set the grand strategy for the prosecution of the war. There was universal agreement on one principle: Germany first. It was obvious that Germany could win the war without Japan, but Japan could not win the war without Germany. The first battle Marshall had to fight (and with mixed success for the next two years) was a core/periphery strategy. Marshall was a tireless advocate of a cross-channel invasion in France and a direct strike into the heart of Germany. Still haunted by the ghosts of the First World War and the Somme (sixty thousand casualties in one day and nearly a million killed in the war), Churchill and his advisors favored a peripheral approach: Norway, North Africa, Sardinia, the Balkans—anything to prolong the invasion of France until Germany's resistance was materially weakened.

Domestically and with the Allies, Marshall won a signal victory, the unified or supreme command he deemed essential. He first convinced the president, then his fellow chiefs, and finally Churchill by suggesting British general Archibald Wavell for the supreme command in the Far East. Harry Hopkins and Max Beaverbrook (the British minister of supply) settled on a civilian board to allocate war production.

Marshall was adamantly opposed, arguing that such a board would have veto power over military operations. The ever-helpful Hopkins reversed himself and worked with Marshall to kill the very plan he coauthored. Marshall at a single stroke modernized the command structure of the army, eliminating the old fiefdoms of infantry, cavalry, field artillery, and coast artillery, replacing them with simple ground forces and supply and air commands.

Pearl Harbor ended the career of Admiral Harold R. (Betty) Stark. In his stead Marshall had to deal with the irascible and volatile Admiral Ernest J. King. With the elevation of Henry (Hap) Arnold, chief of the Army Air Corps, to membership on the Joint Chiefs of Staff, it made two army men versus one navy, a situation likely to set King on the warpath. In a deft stroke Marshall convinced Roosevelt to appoint Admiral William D. Leahy as chief of staff at the White House, while at the same time sitting as chairman of the Joint Chiefs of Staff. Leahy was most cooperative, and Marshall was de facto chairman but to King's mind, at least, not de jure. It was a tough sell with Roosevelt, but by this time Marshall's credibility was soaring.

On December 14, 1941 a newly minted Brigadier General Dwight Eisenhower arrived in Washington at Marshall's summons. It was a giant step for Eisenhower. Marshall, in his opening words, asked Eisenhower how he would deal with the impending disaster in the Philippines and the grave threat to Australia. Two hours later Eisenhower returned with a concise three hundred words. Marshall: "I agree with you. . . . Do your best." On February 6, Marshall named Eisenhower head of the War Plans Division. His job: develop a global strategy. In June Eisenhower was named commander of European Theater Operations.

Circumstances soon conspired to damp Marshall's hopes for a cross-channel invasion. First in late 1942 and soon after,

even in 1943, the arms, troops, and, most importantly, the shipping and landing craft were not there. Roosevelt had one imperative: to bring American troops against the Germans in 1942, an election year. Out of this was born Operation Torch, the three-pronged invasion of North Africa at Casablanca, Oran, and Algiers. In order to neutralize the French, Eisenhower cut a deal with the smarmy Admiral Darlan of the Vichy French government. This rained a firestorm of protest in both the British and American press. Eisenhower was the obvious scapegoat. Had it not been for Marshall's unstinting support this incident might have ended Eisenhower's career.

The Trident Conference in May 1943 aimed to chart the Allied course after North Africa and Sicily. For Marshall the cross-channel invasion—called Operation Roundup— was the obvious choice in the spring of 1944. For Churchill and the British it was anything else, principally a grab bag in the Mediterranean, including an all-out assault on Italy, Rhodes, Greece, and Yugoslavia, what Churchill mistakenly called the "soft underbelly of Europe." These peripheral objectives not only served to postpone Roundup, but denied the critical shipping for Admiral King's Pacific Theater. Marshall agreed to a limited Italian campaign in exchange for a firm May 1, 1944 date for Roundup. It was Marshall who drafted the communiqué to Stalin. In Churchill's words: "He was a statesman with a penetrating and commanding view of the whole scene."

In Algiers Marshall gave a rare press conference. It became an essential part of the Marshall legend. He began by asking each of the thirty correspondents to pose their questions. Marshall remained silent until the last question was posed, and then talked for forty minutes, answering each question, looking directly at its author, and weaving it all into his global portrait. It was a stunning performance, and all of this from a man who rarely gave press conferences.

While still pledged to Roundup (now Operation Overlord) Churchill had resurrected his Eastern Mediterranean strategy. He called attention to the deficiencies of the American fighting man by suggesting that it would take two and one-half U.S. divisions to fight one German division. Marshall exploded: "I never want to hear this again." Churchill backpedaled, but after a good night's sleep Churchill returned to his favorite subject, the invasion of Rhodes. Beginning with "muskets must flame" and more vintage Churchillian rhetoric, he made his case. Marshall fixed Churchill, perhaps the greatest man of the century, straight in the eye and stated flatly: "Not one American boy is going to die on that goddamned beach."

One sidelight of the Cairo Conference concerned the commander of the China, Burma, and India theater, General Joseph L. (Vinegar Joe) Stillwell. Marshall regarded Stillwell as the finest combat soldier in the U.S. army, as opposed to Patton, whom he thought a prima donna. Stillwell, amongst his operational duties, was chief of staff to Chinese leader Chiang Kai-Shek. He thought Chiang was worthless. Privately he called him "peanut." Roosevelt wanted Stillwell out and even sent an emissary to inform Marshall, who promptly sent him back. On the Andaman Islands (off the coast of India) invasion admiral King and chief of the Imperial Staff Alan Brooke went at it. According to Stillwell, "King almost climbed over the table at Brooke. God he was mad. I wish he had socked him." Marshall loved the guy. Roosevelt finally relieved him in October 1944.

Marshall had only one card left to play. What would Stalin's reaction be at Tehran a few days later? Stalin decisively pronounced on Overlord, Italy, and other operations he regarded as only auxiliary. Significant resources would be transferred from the Mediterranean to Bolero for the build-up in Britain for Overlord. In December 1943 *Time* magazine named Marshall "Man of the Year."

Stalin had asked who was to command Overload. Roosevelt and Churchill sheepishly said it was undecided. Stalin, pressing the issue, said that until the supreme commander was announced he doubted the operation would come off. An answer was promised in two weeks. It was universally assumed that it would be Marshall. He wanted the job but would not ask for it. Roosevelt had been long leaning toward Marshall. Two weeks prior to Tehran he told Eisenhower: "Ike, you and I know who was chief of staff during the last years of the Civil War (Henry Halleck—Old Brains) but practically no one else knows. . . . I hate to think that fifty years from now practically nobody will know who George Marshall was." Roosevelt asked the ubiquitous Hopkins to find out from Marshall what he wanted to do. Marshall responded, "I will serve at the pleasure of the president." Roosevelt then posed the question directly to Marshall—same answer. Ironically in the end it was Marshall's staggering accomplishments and Eisenhower's relative inexperience that denied Marshall the job he wanted most. Had Eisenhower gone back as acting chief of staff he would have had problems with the imperious MacArthur under whom he had worked as a major. He would have lacked Marshall's sure touch with the Congress. Marshall had become the indispensable man. Roosevelt made the right decision denying Marshall the job he wanted most and accelerating Eisenhower's trajectory toward the White House.

After D-Day Marshall's principal concern in Europe was to back up Eisenhower's unceasing efforts to counter the prickly British field marshal Bernard Montgomery. During the Battle of the Bulge Eisenhower's confidence had been shaken, and the British argued for the appointment of an overall armed forces commander, obviously British. While disappointed with certain of Eisenhower's actions, Marshall knew Eisenhower and the Americans would lose control of

the theater with a British commander of the armed forces. Marshall wouldn't let it happen. When Churchill appealed directly to Roosevelt, it was Marshall who drafted the president's reply.

President Roosevelt died April 12, 1945. Marshall made the funeral arrangements. From the start, his relationship with Truman was exceptional. As an artillery captain in the first war, Truman was proud of his military service and looked with awe upon the man he was later to call the "greatest military man this country has ever produced." For his part Marshall felt far more confident with the plain-talking Truman than the mercurial Duchess County squire.

Marshall retired from the army on November 26, 1945. The next day Truman appointed him special ambassador to China. His job was to reconcile Chiang Kai-Shek and the Kuomintang with Mao Tse-tung and the communists. Marshall was accustomed to success; however, the China conundrum both militarily and politically was impossible. His mission was a failure. His sympathies with Stilwell's plight only deepened with his agonizing year in China.

In May of 1946 Truman sent Eisenhower (now Army chief of staff) to sound out Marshall about taking over as secretary of state from Jimmy Byrnes. Marshall replied, "Great goodness, Eisenhower, I'd take any job in the world to get out of this one." Marshall was sworn in on January 21, 1947. The selection of Marshall was the best appointment of the Truman presidency. With inflation, labor problems, and the Russian menace, Truman was in deep trouble in 1946; a significant segment of the public was convinced he was not up to the job but they sure as hell knew Marshall was up to his job. The Marshall appointment marked the inflection point of the Truman presidency.

Marshall's first move was to ask Dean Acheson, under secretary of state for Jimmy Byrnes, to stay on. The sophisticated Acheson, with his bristling guardsman's mustache, was

awed by few men. Marshall was the exception. Marshall then named George Frost Kennan, the former chargé d'affaires at the Moscow embassy, as head of the policy planning staff. Kennan was catapulted to prominence with his authorship of the famous "long telegram" in February 1946. In it he identified the expansionist sources of Soviet conduct and defined the policy of containment that undergirded the U.S. response to communism for the duration of the Cold War.

Marshall's first state department crisis broke in February 1947, when a bankrupt Britain announced that it could no longer support the Greek government against the communist insurgency. Truman and Marshall stepped into the breach with a $400 million aid package, which they worked through a recalcitrant Congress only with the heavy efforts of Republican senator Arthur Vandenberg of Michigan. Out of this was born the "Truman Doctrine"—the first tangible results of "containment."

In early 1947 Western Europe was sliding into political and economic chaos; communist strength at the poles was growing. After a series of foreign minister meetings in Moscow, Marshall returned totally disabused of the notion that he could reach any accommodation with the Russians. In June he delivered a commencement speech at Harvard. It was the most important speech he ever gave and for its impact (Marshall was no spellbinder) one of the most important speeches of the twentieth century. In it he announced the European Recovery Plan (ERP), more commonly known as the Marshall Plan. Truman named it the Marshall Plan, rightly reasoning that, regardless of its merits, the Truman Plan would not have made it through the Republican-controlled 80th Congress. Marshall never called it anything other than ERP. Acheson, Kennan, and under secretary for economic affairs Will Clayton hammered out the policy. Marshall presented the plan as one of the most selfless acts in American

history: "Our policy is directed not against any country or doctrine but against hunger, poverty, desperation, and chaos." Truman gave it his unswerving support, but it was Marshall's towering reputation with Arthur Vandenberg and the Congress that made it a reality.

Marshall was opposed to any further aid to nationalist China. His time as Truman's special ambassador in 1946 and 1947 had convinced him that Chiang was doomed to defeat. Concerned about being "sucked into" a land war in Asia, he adamantly opposed further military aid. In the early 1950s he paid a modest price when Senator Joe McCarthy screamed, "Who lost China?" Fingers were pointed at Marshall.

In the face of persistent Russian intransigence Marshall proposed to France and Britain the unification of their German occupation zones. On June 7, 1948, the Allies called for a constituents' assembly to draft a constitution for an independent and unoccupied West Germany. The Russians responded with the Berlin blockade. Contemporaneously Marshall worked toward a U.S.-European military pact. In an uncharacteristic burst of immodesty, Marshall told his biographer Forrest Pogue: "I started NATO. I got every living soul one after the other to talk to me personally on the thing to get them stirred up to do this business."

Right on most things, Marshall on occasion was wrong. One example was the recognition of the State of Israel. Although Truman had already made his decision he heard Marshall out at length. Marshall made a reasoned argument that four hundred thousand Jews could not defeat forty million Arabs. Here Marshall's laser-like focus did him a disservice. A more widely read man might have understood that in this case history might trump military logic. Truman was right. He was concerned that Marshall would resign. He did not, and gave gracious support to his commander in chief.

The third and final act of George Marshall's life was his appointment as the nation's third secretary of defense in September of 1950. The one positive effect of the outbreak of the Korean War was a heightened responsiveness on the part of the Congress and of the American public to the menace of communist aggression. Marshall's prestige gave notable strength to Acheson and his negotiations with the French (prickly as always) over the NATO pact. More important was his unbridled support of the National Security Council Document 68. NSC-68 was drafted by Paul Nitze, Kennan's hard-nosed successor at policy planning. It was the seminal U.S. policy of the Cold War, calling for a vast expansion of American military power throughout the world. It put the teeth into containment. Lastly, Marshall had to deal with a firestorm in the aftermath of Truman's firing of Douglas MacArthur. Marshall, after some deliberation, supported the decision. The man Truman privately called "play actor and bunco man" had clearly overstepped his bounds. Marshall, Bradley, and Acheson suffered through interminable congressional hearings, but in the end the furor just "faded away." Marshall closed his public career in September 1951, just four months short of fifty years.

In 1953 he received the Nobel Peace Prize. His remaining years were spent in contented retirement with his wife Katherine. He died October 16, 1959. The man who had planned the elaborate funerals for presidents Harding and Roosevelt, and General of the Armies Pershing, gave instructions for a simple service.

Greatness rests more easily upon the shoulders of George Marshall than almost any other American. As the nation's longest-serving chief of staff he set the strategy that won World War II. He was the "organizer of victory." As Harry Truman's secretary of state and secretary of defense he set the policies that won the Cold War. As the greatest American of the twentieth century he has but one peer: the ringmaster of Hyde Park.

10

THE BUSINESS OF POLITICS: THE STORY OF DAVID L. LAWRENCE

THE YEAR WAS 1955, THE PLACE THE LONG BAR AT THE Carlton House Hotel. Standing as bookends were Pirates sportscaster Bob (the "Gunner") Prince and KDKA newscaster, curly-haired Bill Burns. Both men were serious drinkers, but the Gunner, resplendent in a canary yellow blazer with an ever-present screwdriver in hand and another awaiting in the on-deck circle, was besting the anchorman two to one. The hum of the conversation warmed as much as the alcohol. The Pittsburgh Renaissance was near high tide and David Leo Lawrence was mayor.

David L. Lawrence (1889–1966) is the foremost political figure this city has produced. He was one of America's major political bosses and machine politicians in a select triumvirate with Boston's James Michael Curley (1874–1958) and Chicago's Richard J. Daley (1902–1976). Lawrence lacked the talent and intellectual capacity of the flamboyant Curley,

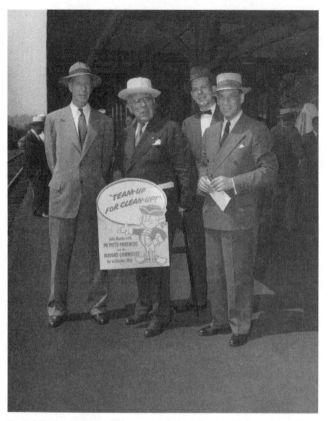

David L. Lawrence. Library and Archives Division, Sen. John
Heinz History Center

although unlike Curley he never logged any jail time. The
closest parallel is with the jowly and ham-fisted Daley. Both
were political bosses throughout most of their careers, accept-
ing the mantle of high political office only deep into middle
age. Lawrence was elected mayor of Pittsburgh in 1945 at age
fifty-six, and Daley became mayor of Chicago in 1955 when he
was fifty-three.

Lawrence's grandparents, Isaac Lawrence and Charles
Conwell, emigrated from Northern Ireland shortly after the
midcentury potato famine. Both families settled near the Fort
Pitt Blockhouse, becoming part of an ethnic subset known as
"Point Irish." Charles B. Lawrence, Isaac's second son, mar-

ried Catherine Conwell, the third of nine girls in 1880. David Lawrence, the youngest of four children, was born in 1889. The Lawrence family was working class; they lived a modest but comfortable existence. Catherine Lawrence was the dominant figure in the household, devoting her energies toward daily observance of her devout Catholic faith. She was no Margaret Carnegie and gave little thought toward upward mobility. Her family life was stable and cohesive; she wanted her children to replicate it by emphasizing employment over education.

David Lawrence's schooling was modest. Elementary school was capped by a two-year commercial course. His education was cut short by lack of scholastic aptitude more than a lack of funds. A half-century later he revealed, "I was no boy wonder in education. It was always a struggle for me." Throughout his life he would remain acutely conscious of his educational deficiencies. He invariably favored the highly educated—in particular, Ivy League graduates—for his key appointments.

Learning the Ropes

In 1903, fourteen-year-old David Lawrence apprenticed himself to attorney William J. Brennan (1856). The association lasted for nearly twenty years until Brennan's death. Born into an Irish working-class family much like Lawrence's, Brennan began work at Jones & Laughlin Steel at age eleven. He read law at night and established a practice in 1883. For Lawrence, the hours were long and the pay meager. In Brennan's small office, legal practice and politics were closely intertwined. The nonacademically inclined Lawrence chose politics over reading law; he read people. Brennan was a lawyer first and a politician second. This gave his young lieutenant the space to develop his political skills.

Today, after nearly eighty years of Democratic dominance in Pittsburgh politics, it is hard to imagine a

time when Pittsburgh was held in the vise-like grip of a Republican machine. The nascent and weak Democratic organization was forced to cooperate within the space granted it by Republican bosses such as William Magee and William Flinn, as they battled fellow Republicans Matthew Quay, Edward Bigelow, and others. Lawrence and Brennan worked slowly and patiently with the Republican overlords, opportunistically exploiting their intraparty battles. At a very early age, Lawrence learned the art of compromise. In reflecting back on these lessons Lawrence remembered, "We are practical people, not ideologists."

No doubt to distance himself from his modest beginnings, Brennan adopted a formal style in both dress and behavior. Lawrence carefully mimicked his mentor. For Lawrence coat, tie, and white shirt with French cuffs became the order of the day. Even at home or at a picnic, informality was signaled by the occasional doffing of his suit coat, but the tie was ever present. As a professional politician Lawrence cast his respect for political office in terms of dress appropriate to the office. When any of the Democratic faithful showed up at Democratic headquarters or Lawrence's office in a short-sleeved shirt or no tie, they were admonished in no uncertain terms—"Goddamn it! You are a gentleman. This is an office."

In 1912 Lawrence attended the Democratic National Convention, accompanying Brennan as a page. On this trip Lawrence met and bonded with a wealthy Westmoreland County Democrat, Joseph Guffey. Guffey—a future U.S. senator—went all out for Woodrow Wilson, whom he had known as a Princeton undergraduate. Wilson rewarded Guffey by naming him Western Pennsylvania patronage chief. Guffey, in turn, appointed Lawrence minority commissioner for voter registration in Pittsburgh. The job paid $4,000 a year and was Lawrence's first salaried political position.

In the absence of massive corruption on the scale of the Marcos regime in the Philippines, the life of the professional politician normally skates along on financially thin ice. In 1916 Lawrence launched an insurance agency with Republican state senator Frank Harris. Lawrence knew little about insurance and was no businessman, but he made a great hire in Jimmy Kirk, who ran the Harris Lawrence Agency until his death in 1945. He was Lawrence's closest confidant. In his later years, the agency provided Lawrence with an income of $15,000 to $20,000 per year, and during his years out of office it provided the bulk of his income.

Standing 5'9" and full-bodied, Lawrence's most distinguishing features were a large head, thick neck, and broad shoulders. Early on his mien and carriage marked him as a man of power. He possessed phenomenal stamina, working twelve- to fifteen-hour days, often seven days a week. Like an athlete in training he took good care of himself. He neither drank nor smoked. He ate moderately and exercised regularly.

His mentor Brennan once told him that, as a politician, you could not "thrive and wive" at the same time. Only in 1922 after Brennan's death did Lawrence marry at age thirty-two. Alyce Golden, the seventh child of Irish immigrants, was seven years younger than Lawrence. They had five surviving children, three boys and two girls. Lawrence was an absentee father and husband. Alyce shouldered the full burden of raising the family.

Again, at the 1920 Democratic convention, a Guffey connection paid dividends for Lawrence. For services rendered Guffey was named Democratic national committeeman from Pennsylvania. He then appointed Lawrence to his old job as Allegheny County Democratic chairman. This was not initially a position of power, as the Democrats would remain in the political wilderness for another twelve years until Roosevelt's victory in 1932, but, characteristically, Lawrence painstakingly

put together a Democratic organization to fill the minority positions to which it was entitled. When the pendulum finally swung in his party's direction, Lawrence's nascent organization would propel Democratic candidates into office across the board making him the most powerful Democrat in Pennsylvania.

The 1932 Democratic Convention was Lawrence's most important yet, but he still played second fiddle to his powerful sponsor, Joseph Guffey. His heart was still with the 1928 candidate, New York's Al Smith, but his head was with New York governor Franklin D. Roosevelt. He was convinced that Smith's Catholicism doomed his electoral prospects.

Going into the convention FDR could count on only a few big city bosses, notably Ed Crump from Memphis, Tom Pendergast of Kansas City, and the Bronx's Ed Flynn. Lawrence at that time was not in their league, but in conjunction with Guffey he went all out for Roosevelt. They were able to deliver fifty-five votes on four ballots, more than those of any other state.

Lawrence then worked feverishly to bring both Pittsburgh and Pennsylvania into the Roosevelt column. With his firm grip on Pittsburgh's thirty-two wards, he focused on ethnic minorities including the Irish, Italians, Polish, and other eastern and southern Europeans. His success with blacks was notable. Robert Vann, the editor of the nationally distributed black newspaper the *Pittsburgh Courier,* a long-time Republican as were most blacks since the Civil War, had gotten repeated short-shrift from the dominant Republican machine. Lawrence was able to secure an audience for Vann with FDR at his home in Hyde Park, New York. Vann was soon won over by the high-voltage Roosevelt charm. He brought home the bacon for the Democrats in Pittsburgh's black wards and helped the ticket nationally. Lawrence then shored up his party's finances by convinc-

ing some long-time Republican money men to shift to Roosevelt. Capping this fundraising effort was a $50,000 contribution from the great oil wildcatter, Mike Benedum. At Lawrence's urging, FDR came to Pittsburgh. Lawrence gambled by leasing Forbes Field with thirty-five thousand seats. Fifty thousand ended up cramming the ballpark. As a master stroke, Lawrence had Mike Benedum introduce the candidate.

In 1932 Roosevelt failed to carry Pennsylvania. The shortfall was in Philadelphia. He won Pittsburgh by twenty-seven thousand votes and carried twenty-seven out of thirty-two wards. FDR was prompt in rewarding Guffey and Lawrence. Guffey, the state's top Democrat, was given control of all federal patronage in Pennsylvania. He in turn delegated control in Western Pennsylvania to Lawrence.

He moved with dispatch to harvest the cornucopia of opportunities presented by the Roosevelt victory. Putting aside calls to be the Democratic mayoralty candidate in 1933, he chose Protestant blueblood William McNair. He also ran the campaign, hammering home ad nauseam McNair as the Roosevelt candidate for mayor, causing the *New York Times* to observe that "one might think that it was Mr. Roosevelt that is running for mayor." McNair won handily, but this was just the start.

In 1936, in addition to the mayor's office, the Democrats controlled the county board of commissioners and held all nine seats on the city council and most of the elected row offices. George H. Earle was elected governor and appointed Lawrence as secretary of the Commonwealth, a dominant position in the state administration. With Guffey in the Senate and conveniently out of Pennsylvania, Lawrence, who had been named Democratic state chairman in 1934, now held undisputed dominion over statewide Pennsylvania patronage. The fortunes of the Pennsylvania Democratic

Party would remain under his sway until his death in 1966. He was now "Boss Lawrence," a position he long desired, but a moniker he thoroughly disliked.

The Lawrence Machine

Former House Speaker Thomas P. "Tip" O'Neill famously declared that "all politics are local." Nowhere was this more true than with the operations of the Lawrence machine in Pittsburgh. Even as he rose to regional, state, and national prominence, his political power rested on a bedrock of local politics. Let's go down into the engine room and see how the machine worked.

Pittsburgh (1940 population: 676,000) was divided into thirty-two wards. The ward voters elected a committee, its chairman charged with maximizing the party's votes on election day. The coin of the realm for the ward chairman was political patronage—jobs. In 1936, Lawrence, the state Democratic chairman, had nearly total control over 150,000 federal jobs, including 57,000 in Western Pennsylvania. Once a ward chairman secured a job for one of his constituents, the new and thankful job holder (in the depths of the Depression a job was a dear thing) was expected to secure votes from family, friends, neighbors, and coworkers for the upcoming election. On top of all this were county, state, and federal jobs. They provided the dominant Democratic Party with a powerful and virtually unbeatable arsenal in the election campaigns ahead. On election day, public employees were urged to be at the polls checking off the votes they pledged to deliver. They were also expected to commit money in modest sums, as well as their time.

The ward chairman was the point person for all Lawrence's initiatives. Any job petitioner approaching Lawrence was politely but firmly directed to his appropriate ward. By 1936 this well-oiled system had eight hundred

policemen and one thousand firemen holding their jobs through the sufferance of their ward leadership.

Lawrence both derived and exercised his power through the ward chairmen. His relationship with the chairmen varied with their ability to deliver votes. Some highly successful chairmen ran virtually independent fiefdoms, while those with shortcomings felt Lawrence's hot breath on their neck all too often. When the chairman of a South Side ward was called on the carpet for his failure to deliver his quota of Democrats, he responded that it had rained all day. Lawrence, "How the hell do you think the weather was on the North Side?" When called on the carpet for a barely legible announcement, the responsible individual complained that his copy machine was not working properly. On this one Lawrence cut loose with both barrels: "Don't ever send me a thing like this again. Most of all you can't read it. Second it makes no sense. I'm near blind in one eye and I don't want to lose the other."

The formal structure of the party organization fit comfortably Lawrence's proclivity for regularity and orderliness. Unlike Chicago's Richard Daley, Lawrence seldom met individual citizens or small groups at City Hall. But in support of ward politics Lawrence was ever visible at sporting events, weddings, and funerals. More than once he said, "Visit the sick and bury the dead." Charisma is not a word one would apply to Lawrence. He was well removed from the backslapping style of Boston's Michael Curley and New York's mayor Fiorello H. LaGuardia. He was at best a fair public speaker. An associate once observed you could always tell when Lawrence found a new word. He would beat it to death. One time it was "sanguine." For the next few months he was invariably sanguine about this and not sanguine about that. Despite his natural reserve and "all business" personality, David Lawrence won the hearts and minds of

the citizens of Pittsburgh. In a blue-collar town, he was the blue-collar leader. With his working-class background, despite his formal appearance and demeanor, he was always one of "them."

Choosing the appropriate Democratic candidates for office was always a top priority for Lawrence. At "slating caucuses" in his Benedum Trees office, Lawrence spent countless hours working with Democratic Party leaders to hammer out a winning slate. An acceptable candidate who could win was invariably chosen over an outstanding candidate whose vote-getting ability might be suspect. The party always came first and the performance of the successful officeholder came second. Many times a solid vote getter and an effective officeholder were one and the same. But all too often mediocrity triumphed at the polls; this was simply a fact of life with machine politics. The priorities were to, one, build the party; two, win elections; and, three, dispense patronage, which in turn built the party. This was the three-cycle engine that powered the Lawrence machine.

The all-consuming nature of politics in general and Lawrence's brand in particular was shown in the way he administered his Pittsburgh fiefdom after assuming the duties of secretary of the Commonwealth. He caught the Friday 3:00 p.m. train from Harrisburg, arriving in Pittsburgh after 8:00 p.m. On Saturdays he was in his Benedum Trees office by 10:00 a.m. After two hours devoted to urgent business with his inner circle, he met the ward chairmen, reviewing the minutest details of ward politics. He seldom left before 6:00 p.m. On Sunday he attended 10:00 a.m. Mass at St. Mary's at the Point. His duties as an usher permitted him to hold court in the back of the church. By noontime he would return to his office for a shortened reprise of Saturday's schedule. On slow days he might summon his pinochle cronies for some well-deserved relaxation.

The liberal legislation that Earle and Lawrence hoped to pass only became a reality after the sweeping Roosevelt victory in 1936. With Democrats firmly in control of both houses of the legislature, they quickly passed the most liberal legislation the state had ever seen. It was called the "little New Deal." Unfortunately for Lawrence the honeymoon was to be short lived. From 1938 to 1944 he would wander in a political desert.

In and Out of the Desert

Troubles began with the 1938 state elections. Governor Earle could not succeed himself and ran for the Senate. Lawrence selected Allegheny County solicitor Charles Alvin Jones. A Protestant, Jones was one of Lawrence's weaker choices. Lawrence seemed convinced that Catholic candidates labored under a serious handicap. Guffey supported a rival candidate in the primary, adding to the growing breach with Lawrence. Both Jones and Earle (running for the Senate) went down to defeat.

For Lawrence political failure was coupled with the threat of jail time. In 1939 he was indicted and acquitted of taking kickbacks from an aggregates company. In 1940 he was forced to run the gauntlet again. This time he was charged with threatening state employees (macing) to extract political contributions. Two years of constant litigation took their toll on Lawrence and his family. In addition to Lawrence's other problems, tragedy struck in 1942 when his two oldest sons, David, Jr. and William Brennan Lawrence, were killed in an automobile accident.

The blame for the Guffey/Lawrence split must be shared by both parties. At its core, doubtless, was some jealousy on the part of the master with his student's growing prominence. On Lawrence's side, he violated his cardinal rule of compromise with his virulent attacks on Guffey in the 1940

Democratic primary. Guffey won and wanted Lawrence out as state chairman. Bowing to party pressure, Lawrence resigned but did manage to secure the position of Democratic national committeeman as part of the deal. This brought Lawrence into national prominence over the next two decades. At the Democratic National Convention in Chicago in 1944, Lawrence was among a handful of Democratic powerbrokers who helped secure the nomination for Harry Truman.

Lawrence began his political comeback with the victory of his candidate, F. Clair Ross, over Guffey's choice of Judge Ralph Smith in the 1942 Democratic primary. The victory over Guffey soon propelled Lawrence back into his old position of Democratic state chairman. Riding Roosevelt's coattails, Lawrence led the Democratic slate to a clean sweep in the 1944 election.

Cornelius B. Scully, an Episcopalian, had been the mayor of Pittsburgh since 1936. Handpicked by Lawrence, Scully proved to be a competent mayor, but barely eked out a victory in the 1941 mayoralty elections. In 1945 the party was convinced they needed a replacement for the lackluster vote getter.

The first choice of the party hierarchy was three-term county commissioner John Kane. But Kane's powerbase was in Allegheny County, not in the city. He was reluctant to abandon it to play second fiddle to Lawrence. Instead he marshaled the leadership to promote a Lawrence candidacy. Arguing against his own draft, Lawrence listed three strikes against him, his highly publicized trials, the public's innate distrust of professional politicians, and last as always his Catholicism. Finally Lawrence acquiesced, and the formidable Kane agreed to be his campaign manager. Lawrence defeated his Republican opponent, Robert Wadell, by a modest fourteen thousand votes. It was his first electoral victory in a thirty-year career. In his subsequent campaigns, his election was never in doubt.

The Renaissance

In 1945 Pittsburgh was a rundown and tired city. Mayor-elect Lawrence faced a daunting host of problems. His old neighborhood in the Point was a tangled rabbit-warren of warehouses and railroad tracks. The last major office building erected was the forty-story Gulf Building in 1932; none were planned for the postwar period. Between 1900 and 1945 there were five floods including the catastrophic flood of 1936, which left half of the commercial section of the city under eleven feet of water. Even worse were the smoke and smog caused by a combination of the belching steel mills and 142,000 homes heated by soft coal. On many mornings by 9:00 a.m. the sky was pitch black and the city was ablaze with headlights and neon signs. Many of the city's major corporations were making plans to move their headquarters to more accommodating environments.

David L. Lawrence, during his thirteen years in the mayor's office (1946–1959), was a guiding force in the transformation of the city in what was called the Pittsburgh Renaissance—a self-awarded title. The two principal thrusts of the Pittsburgh Renaissance were cleaning the air and rebuilding a decaying downtown.

Lawrence was fortunate to have a dedicated business partner in Richard King Mellon, the son of R. B. Mellon and the grandson of the Judge. Mellon, chairman of Mellon National Bank, was the richest and most influential leader of the Pittsburgh business community. Neither could have done it alone, but Lawrence was the first mover. His broad-brush plan for city revitalization found a receptive ear in General Mellon. The vehicle that brought them together was the Allegheny Conference on Community Development, sponsored by Mellon in 1944. Far more so than today, Pittsburgh was a company town—the third-largest headquarters city in the United States. Twenty or so members of the executive

committee of the conference were the CEOs of the city's major corporations. Once agreed upon a course of action, when the conference and General Mellon said "march," the business community marched.

Within twenty-four hours of his election Lawrence announced his campaign against air pollution. His statewide political power forced through the required air quality legislation, while the conference beat back any recalcitrance on the part of the steel industry. Lawrence delegated more power to his executive secretary John T. Robin than any of his previous aides. Robin, in turn, worked with Mellon's man Arthur Van Buskirk to keep the political and business teams in harness.

Until 1946 Mellon and Lawrence had not met. At Arthur Van Buskirk's urging, Mellon made the brief walk across Grant Street to the mayor's office. After years of battling Mellon's older cousin W. L. Mellon, the meeting doubtless had a surreal quality for Lawrence. The dynamic Lawrence and the laid-back Mellon were opposites in personality, as well as background. This odd couple never became friends, but their shared love of their native city created a force that drove all else before it.

During the 1930s there had been plans to create a park at the Point and surround it with much needed office space. The project languished until the catalyst of a spectacular fire on March 9, 1946. The way was now opened to make the Point State Park and Gateway Center development a reality. The public/private instrument for urban renewal was the Urban Development Authority of Pittsburgh (URA), which held its first meeting in November. Lawrence intended to appoint Arthur Van Buskirk, the chairman of the Allegheny Conference, as head of the URA. Van Buskirk, however, had a better idea: Lawrence as chairman. At first reluctant, the mayor agreed on the condition that Van Buskirk serve as vice chair along with two other conference members.

The Equitable Life Assurance Company of America developed the Gateway project, which began with three twenty-four-story office towers bordering Point State Park. Negotiations took four years, with construction beginning in 1950. Seven major corporations moved their headquarters into the new space. URA purchased the Jones & Laughlin Steel Building, permitting the company to move to Gateway. This was one of numerous URA initiatives under Lawrence's guiding hand that made the vision of the urban planners a reality. The Mellon Square project followed shortly after. During a fifteen-year period, the Pittsburgh Renaissance transformed over one thousand acres in sixteen projects. Over $622 million went into these initiatives, including $500 million of private investment.

The Pittsburgh Renaissance was in part greased by steady corruption, occasionally punctuated by headline-grabbing scandal. Ground zero for this corruption was the police department. Lawrence tacitly supported what he might have termed "low-level corruption." He opposed a state law placing detectives and inspectors under civil service control. All-night bars, gambling establishments, and the numbers rackets flourished throughout the Lawrence years. The best example of his indulgence of criminal activity was his steadfast refusal, despite badgering by several members of his executive staff, to fire police superintendent Harvey Scott, who had held the job since 1939. When the heat from the press became unbearable, he called Scott and his senior officers in and read them the riot act; nothing changed. Finally Scott was hoisted by his own petard. In 1952, within a two-month period, he appeared intoxicated at a grand jury hearing and engaged in a brawl at a restaurant. Having no choice, Lawrence replaced him with an energetic young Jim Slusser, who made marked progress in reducing police corruption.

But even the hard-driving Slusser had to work against political headwinds. The day after his appointment a man

walked into his office and announced he was Slusser's
new inspector. Slusser threw him out, and within hours
Lawrence called and informed him that the man had
received his appointment through his ward chairman and
ordered him reinstated. These actions and others like it
were indelibly stamped on Lawrence's forty-year behav-
ior pattern. His ability to get things done, most specifi-
cally his herculean efforts on behalf of the Pittsburgh
Renaissance, rested on the grassroots support he enjoyed in
the wards. A corruption-free police force simply did not fit
into Lawrence's modus operandi.

A nominal capstone to David Lawrence's political career
was his election as governor in 1957. It was a position he
neither desired nor sought. His great work over thirteen
years in Pittsburgh, as well his prominence on the national
level, both overshadowed his four years (1959–1963) in
Harrisburg. Lawrence's strong desire was to finish his final
term as Pittsburgh mayor. But when Democratic gover-
nor George Leader found himself at cross purposes with
the powers in Philadelphia, Lawrence was the only man
left standing. He narrowly defeated the pretzel king from
Reading, Pennsylvania, Arthur T. McGonigle. Three weeks
before the end of his term, President Kennedy offered him
a job as chairman of the President's Committee on Equal
Opportunity in Housing. It was a subject in which he had a
keen interest and offered a new challenge in a new environ-
ment. He accepted and served in that capacity under presi-
dents Kennedy and Johnson until his death in 1966.

Although Lawrence spent considerable time in
Pittsburgh—he still chaired the URA—the Lawrence
machine was no longer firing on all cylinders. Bearing wit-
ness to this was the defeat of the organization candidate
Bob Casey by the wealthy Philadelphia electronics manu-
facturer Milton Shapp. The Independent Shapp was smart

enough to know that he needed Lawrence and the party organization. He sought rapprochement and Lawrence accommodated him.

On Friday evening, November 4, 1966, Lawrence spoke on behalf of Shapp at the Syria Mosque in Oakland. While at the lectern the seventy-seven-year-old Lawrence was felled by a heart attack. He lingered on at Presbyterian University Hospital for seventeen days but never recovered consciousness. Only a month earlier he had told *Press* writer Kap Monahan, "Don't retire—don't think of it. Keep on at your work and, when your time comes, why not die in harness?" He did just that.

How did David Lawrence accomplish so much? He was a professional at the highest level. He was not an intellectual. He was not an ideologue. He was an "action man" who got the job done. At the heart of his profession was selecting people. Different rules applied to specific categories. Rank and file workers were selected through the normal patronage process. Candidates for office were chosen on their vote-getting capacity. Ability and training were of secondary importance. Top administrative appointments were chosen by education, experience, and ability. Categories one and two were the foundation upon which category three rested.

Lawrence was an outstanding leader. His commitment of both time and intensity was nearly total. His meetings, seldom lasting more than fifteen minutes, were sharp and to the point. Invariably they concluded with a clap of his hands, or a bang of his large ring on the desk. There was never a joke to lighten the mood. His sense of humor on a scale of one to ten was just south of one. He was punctual to a fault. Running for governor in 1957, his running mate John Davis was habitually late. Once, appearing on the same platform with Davis, Lawrence cooled his heels for fifteen minutes. When called out on his tardiness, Davis replied,

"I'm only fifteen minutes late." Lawrence blasted back: "You are fifteen minutes too goddamn late" and walked off the platform.

An aide once described Lawrence as a "nice Lyndon Johnson." This is hardly high praise, but there are similarities. His legacy is all around us today in America's most livable city.

11

THE FOUNDER: THOMAS DETRE AND THE TRANSFORMATION OF HEALTHCARE IN PITTSBURGH

HUNGARY'S PREWAR POPULATION OF SEVEN HUNDRED thousand Jews remained largely unscathed until the spring of 1944. Until then Admiral Nicholas Horthy, the Hungarian Regent, had successfully resisted Hitler's calls for the deportation of Hungarian Jews into the killing maw at Auschwitz/Birkenau, 175 miles due north of Budapest. On March 19, 1944 Hitler ordered the Wehrmacht to occupy Hungary. By July 14, 437,000 Hungarian Jews had been deported to Auschwitz and certain death. The SS continued to round up the remaining pockets of Jews until the red army captured Budapest in February 1945.

One such roundup occurred on November 13, 1944. In one line were those with a Schutz-Pass, a document issued by the Swedish diplomat Raoul Wallenberg, placing them under the tenuous protection of the Swedish government. In a second line were those marked for deportation and death.

In the second line stood twenty-year-old Tamás Feldmeier (later Thomas Detre). A half dozen machine gun toting Hungarian fascists marshaled the helpless Jews. For an hour young Tamás intently watched the half-dozen guards, like a safecracker listening to the tumblers falling into place. Sometimes six pairs of eyes were on him, sometimes three. Then it was two, then one, and for a split second none. In an instant he crossed four steps over to the Schutz-Pass line and gained a reprieve from death.

Thomas Detre. Courtesy of UPMC

Tamás Feldmeier was born in Budapest, the only child of Geza and Gabriella Feldmeier. His father was a German-trained obstetrician-gynecologist. The Feldmeier household was an intellectual hothouse; they seldom dined alone. Through a succession of Austrian and German *fräuleins* (governesses), Tom's first language was German, not Hungarian. Tom was precocious in several dimensions; he began to smoke at age twelve and, after reading several books on Freud, he decided to become a psychiatrist at age fourteen. "My father was upset. He wanted me to be a 'decent doctor,' not a psychiatrist."

Early in the war Tom became convinced that his parents must leave Hungary. Dr. Feldmeier thought otherwise. A decorated officer in the Hungarian Hussars in the First World War, he like other Germans and Austrians thought he would be excepted. He was wrong. Tom's parents, as well as twenty relatives, were murdered at Auschwitz.

Soon after the Russian liberation in 1945, Tom enrolled at the Pázmány Peter University of Science in Budapest. Like many other Holocaust survivors he changed the German Feldmeier to Detre. In French it means appropriately "to live."

Ironically, while it was Sigmund Freud who gave Tom Detre the impetus to pursue a career in psychiatry, he soon turned against psychoanalysis—a theory and subset of psychotherapy. Lengthy sessions between the patient and the psychoanalyst attempt to bring preconscious and subconscious material into consciousness. In Tom's mind there were two serious strikes against psychoanalysis. First, if the disease is neurologically/biologically based, no amount of talking will effect a cure. Second, in those limited cases where analysis may have positive outcomes, it is prohibitively expensive. All this is not to gainsay Sigmund Freud's position as one of the seminal thinkers in the twentieth century. His is perhaps the only other name that may be mentioned in the same breath

as Einstein. However, Freudian psychoanalysis occupies only a small portion of his vast body of thought. In 1946 at twenty-two years of age, Tom was convinced that the future of psychiatry lay in psychopharmacology—the treatment of mental disease through drugs. Non-Freudian psychotherapy was often a necessary adjunct of appropriate psychiatric treatment. He would stake his future career on these convictions.

Tom distinguished himself academically, while at the same time taking increasingly responsible, if temporary, positions at the state mental hospital. For a six-month period at the age of twenty-three he served as the acting director of the state mental hospital. While serving in that capacity on May 1, 1947 he was ordered by a Communist Party official to put on his white coat and march in the May Day worker's parade. His answer was less than politic: "If all the crazies are outside marching, who will take care of the crazies inside?" He promptly received an invitation (no refusals accepted) to visit the headquarters of the Communist Party's secret police. Fortunately Tom Detre never lacked for luck. The hearing officer to which he was assigned turned out to be a former lover. "Darling, this is not the place for you. You have too big a mouth. Make every effort to get out." The May Day incident was hardly a lone event. There were several prior examples of his recalcitrance. He described himself as a serial dissident. Dissenters would have their day but not for another thirty years.

Having narrowly escaped the Nazis, Tom now needed to breach the Iron Curtain. A cousin who was a friend of the Italian ambassador advised Tom that, if he could get an appointment at an Italian university, he would arrange for a visa. Tom had recently written a provocative paper on electroshock therapy. He sent the paper to the noted neurologist Ugo Cerletti, the coinventor of electroconvulsive therapy. The invitation was forthcoming and Tom was off to Rome.

He was in Italy for six years from 1947 to 1953. He completed his education while working at the Italian National Research Council. At the same time he developed a lucrative private practice. The Italian years were good ones for Tom: "You've probably seen the movie *La Dolce Vita.* That was the period I lived in Rome—the late 1940s and early 1950s. I had a good time!" What Tom is telling us here in a not so roundabout way is that the legendary Detre charm, which was later employed with such telling effect on Pittsburgh's power brokers, was given an early trial run with a bevy of attractive young Italian women. The results were positive.

Again with the help of some cousins Tom made it to the United States on May 13, 1953. He spent one year at City Hospital and a second at Mt. Sinai in New York City. Neither was a university hospital, and Tom was much more comfortable in an academic environment. He even turned down a $12,000 job offer (a handsome sum in those days) as a resident in Hawaii, but we can hardly see Tom hanging ten on the surf at Waikiki beach. One of his supervisors at Sinai, a Yale graduate, recommended him to the chairman of the psychiatry department at Yale. "He claimed I was very bright, very industrious, and even funny." Tom was hired as a second-year resident.

In 1956 he married Katherine Maria Dreschler, like himself a Hungarian Jewish refugee. Katherine Detre MD, DrPH, became one of the nation's foremost epidemiologists. In 2000 she received a $52 million grant to study the efficacy of surgery as opposed to nonsurgical treatment for cardiovascular disease. At the time it was the largest National Institutes of Health (NIH) grant ever received by the University of Pittsburgh. This was a fifty-year marriage and romance.

Tom Detre is a change agent. His accomplishments during the Yale years were made in an environment not amenable to the direction in which he wanted to drive the treatment

of the mentally ill. The chairman of the Yale Department of Psychiatry, Frederick C. Redlich, was an analyst along with 75 percent of psychiatry department chairs in the United States. Fortunately, he had sympathy with some of Tom's thinking on the future of psychiatry.

Despite the dominant psychoanalytical orientation of the department, Tom forged ahead. He began to prescribe treatments with antipsychotic drugs (just introduced in the early 1950s) coupled with nonpsychoanalytic psychotherapy. With mild depression, psychotherapy alone may be sufficient to effect a cure. For more severe cases requiring psycho-pharmacological (drug) treatment, psychotherapy is often a necessary adjunct to ensure that the patient follows a specific drug protocol.

In 1960 Tom anticipated the direction of mental health by forming Tompkins I, an experimental psychiatric unit at Yale New Haven Hospital. The premise behind Tompkins I was to prescribe short-term treatment to acutely ill psychotic patients. Long-term care would then be provided on an out-patient basis. Institutionalization of the mentally ill was at best very expensive, not efficacious, and occasionally cruel. "The only purpose of a hospital, as I see it, is to end hospitalization . . . and then to [treat] . . . long-term illness on an outpatient basis." In a word this was the deinstitutionalization of the mentally ill. In the next twenty years it would become part of the cannon of psychiatry.

In addition to psychopharmacology and deinstitu-tionalization, the third element of Tom Detre's pioneering approach to psychiatry was research. Early on Tom believed that the best psychiatric care couldn't be provided in the absence of major academic research. He was convinced that you needed a cutting-edge research effort to deliver the best clinical care; in turn the clinical experience cycled back against research by providing validation for new treatments.

Research and clinical care must not only exist side by side but they must be integrated.

By 1972 Tom was at the top of his field. He was psychiatrist-in-chief at the Yale New Haven Hospital and a tenured full professor. In 1971 he coauthored the influential and controversial 733-page *Modern Psychiatric Treatment.* According to Loren Roth MD, MPH, former chief medical officer at University of Pittsburgh Medical Center (UPMC): "It was the first book to systematically review all potential psychiatric drug treatments and the understanding of the physiological bases of mental illness." Tom commented: "I am only glad that I got my professorship before it came out. Its tone is so provocative they will kill me for it." Tom's path-breaking work would eventually change psychiatry at Yale, but psychoanalytic headwinds would make it slow going. He was ready for a new challenge.

The University of Pittsburgh had two strikes against it when attempting to recruit top caliber talent like Tom Detre. First it was in Pittsburgh, which in those days conjured up the image of the smoke and smog of the early 1940s, when by 9:00 a.m. the sky was pitch black. By 1950 the skies were clean, but the perception lingered on for another fifty years. Secondly, as an academic medical center the university was a clear laggard. Despite having a rich heritage in banner names such as Benjamin Spock, the authority on child development for two generations of mothers, and, most notably, Jonas Salk, the conqueror of polio, they had since departed. Pitt ranked a lowly thirty-seventh in NIH funding. While the upper campus did contain an impressive array of hospitals: Eye & Ear, Children's, Falk Clinic, Magee Women's, and the bell cow, Presbyterian Hospital, they were not academic hospitals. The two leading lights of the university when Tom Detre arrived were strange bedfellows, the nation's number one–ranked philosophy department and Pitt's soon-to-be national championship football team. It is not likely that many football players majored in philosophy.

On the upper campus the state-owned Western State Psychiatric Hospital had opened its doors in 1942. In 1949 the commonwealth effectively transferred ownership of the renamed Western Psychiatric Institute and Clinic (WPIC) to the university. WPIC was an academic hospital in name only. The psychiatry department as well was an also-ran; most of the faculty were private physicians. The commonwealth's funding for WPIC was in jeopardy. State officials were unhappy and regarded WPIC management as arrogant and in conflict with the state's welfare mandate.

As the state threatened to cut funding, academic leaders F. Sargent Cheever MD and the vice chancellor of the Schools of the Health Professions and medical school dean, Donald Medearis, with the full backing of Chancellor Wesley W. Posvar, rose to the occasion. Their twin aims were to make WPIC more responsive to the state and to strengthen biological psychiatry. They successfully appealed to the R. K. Mellon Foundation for a $5 million grant to attract a transformative chairman for the department of psychiatry.

Tom visited Pitt and sized up the situation as requiring radical change. He then wrote Sarge Cheever a four-page, single-spaced letter outlining his plan and his demands. Sarge told Tom he wanted a lot. He answered with a little doggerel: "I am too vain to go down the drain. If you want me to do something you have to provide the resources."

Tom Detre became chairman of the department of psychiatry at the University of Pittsburgh on March 1, 1973. He made several trips to Pittsburgh to start the ball rolling six months before he officially assumed his duties. Tom's first major recruit was thirty-one-year-old David Kupfer as director of research. An assistant professor from Yale, David's resume was a little thin for the job but this shortcoming was mitigated by the fact that there was little research going on at WPIC. Although David and his family didn't particularly want

to come to Pittsburgh, Franco Harris helped out on this one. David saw the Steelers/Oakland Raiders playoff game and Franco's "immaculate reception." Like Moses and the burning bush David regarded it as a sign. He announced to his family: "We're going to Pittsburgh." How good a recruit was David? In 1983 he succeeded Tom as chairman of the psychiatry department and made it the number one recipient of NIH funding—in other words, the best psychiatry department in the United States.

No sooner had Tom walked in the door than the state cut WPIC's appropriation in half from $2.5 million to $1.2 million. With the help of the university's capable lobbyist, Tom went to Harrisburg. He didn't ask for anything; he only asked how he could help. His parting words were: "If you get sick come to us. Here's my telephone number. If you forget it I'm in the telephone book." Detre's charm worked its magic. The cuts were rescinded and the appropriation increased to $3 million.

Tom Detre was arguably the most important recruit in the two-hundred-year history of the University of Pittsburgh. Tom's vision of a leading department of psychiatry for the university and for WPIC rested upon great clinicians and researchers. Oftentimes they are one and the same. But to recruit you have to have money. How did Tom do it? How important is recruiting? Tom: "The most important thing"—hands down.

A university is about the creation and dissemination of knowledge, and of course the creation comes first. The true fixed assets of the academy are not bricks and mortar but the resident scholars. In a less than stellar university or department you have mostly "B" players and some "Cs." Building a preeminent department or university is at best a torturous process. First you have to seed your scholars with an occasional "A" or two—David Kupfer is a case in point. The "As"

then attract more "As" and finally predominate over the diminishing number of "Bs." This is precisely what Tom Detre did. It sounds simple, but before you recruit you have to have money—lots of it. In 1973 the cupboards were bare.

Along with state funding the two revenue streams flowing into WPIC were clinical income and research grants. Clinical revenues were enhanced by two changes. That portion of the clinical income that had previously been returned to the School of Medicine was now retained in the department of psychiatry. As Jeff Romoff tells it: "Our ability to keep that clinical money was one of the great concepts in our history." Soon after a 20 percent tax was placed upon all clinical income. At first blush this might seem to be a zero sum game, more for the department and less for the doctors. It didn't work out that way for two reasons. As great researchers and talented clinicians came into the department they attracted more patients, giving them more clinical revenues. The revenue pie was further increased by reimbursement optimization. George Huber, a Romoff recruit formerly with Blue Cross, understood every nuance of the complex subject of reimbursement: "We employed every legal reimbursement optimization strategy we could." Soon not a nickel was left on the table. All this turned into a win/win for the clinicians and for the department.

On the research side indirect costs were retained in the department rather than being returned to the School of Medicine. As more outstanding researchers came into the department research grants increased, making more funds available for further recruiting. These changes created a self-funding mechanism that fed upon itself in a virtuous cycle. It integrated patient care, research, and education. One might liken this to the creation of the Triborough Bridge Authority by New York's master builder Robert Moses (don't blanch at the comparison). Those toll dollars, safe from the hands of

the politicians, were used to dot New York City with a cornucopia of beneficial projects.

Tom Detre's recruiting record looks a little like Ty Cobb's batting average. Beyond all doubt the best recruit Tom ever made in a galaxy of stars was Jeff Romoff. Talking about Jeff as the trailing spouse stretches the truth a little bit, although Tom's initial interest did center on Jeff's wife Vivian who was the chief psychiatric nurse at Yale New Haven Hospital. Jeff (then twenty-seven) worked for a small mental health counseling group in Waterbury, Connecticut. He sent Tom a plan he had written for a community health center seeking a federal grant. "I read it and decided he was a very bright man, and I knew exactly what I wanted to do with him after I talked to him."

Jeff was hired to head up the newly created Office of Education and Regional Programming (OERP). The mandate of OERP was to provide consulting services for mental health providers throughout Western Pennsylvania. The mental health providers received expertise that they could get nowhere else; its efforts won great plaudits from the commonwealth. Two years later Jeff was named executive director and Tom Detre's right-hand man at WPIC; he was on his way.

During the transformation of WPIC there were potholes all along the way. Tom was shocked by the work habits of the part-time faculty. They ambled in at about 9:30 a.m., had a leisurely coffee break, and then lunch. After lunch: "You couldn't find a Gin Rummy partner, let alone four for a bridge game." Soon all that changed.

Tom once again had to confront his old bugaboo—the psychoanalysts. He insisted they do clinical research on the value of their services; they refused. Tom invited them to appoint a director with a strong research background. Again they refused and took their dispute public in an attempt to discredit Tom and embarrass the university. In this latter

effort they partially succeeded, but, with strong backing from Sarge Cheever and Wes Posvar, Tom prevailed. In 1976 the Psychoanalytic Institute withdrew from the university.

From 1973 to 1983 the money came in and the talent followed; WPIC was transformed. In 1977 WPIC was given the prestigious designation as a Clinical Research Center for Affective Disorders by the National Institute of Mental Health. NIH research grants increased from $450,000 in 1973 to $9.5 million in 1983. That year it ranked number three in NIH grants for psychiatric research. NIH grants in psychiatry, as well as all academic medicine, constitute the gold standard of competitive validation. To house its burgeoning research capacity WPIC opened its $6 million, ten-story Education and Research Center in 1982. Full-time faculty increased over fourfold from thirty-six to one hundred and fifty.

By 1982 Tom Detre had reached a crossroads. His national reputation was attracting a number of impressive job offers, including the chair of the psychiatry department at Columbia University. His ten years at WPIC had not been easy; he battled stiff headwinds all the way. If he moved to another department of psychiatry trumpets would herald his arrival. It was a siren song of no little appeal. Wes Posvar knew he had a leader of inestimable value in Tom Detre. Stepping into the breach was a very helpful ally, Nathan Stark, the health policy lawyer who served as senior vice chancellor for health sciences since 1974. He had worked closely with Tom and shared Wes's high opinion of his value to the future of the health sciences at Pitt. He was ready to retire in a year. Posvar and Stark laid out a clear path for Tom to become senior vice chancellor of the health sciences—and soon. It was an offer Tom could not refuse. On October 6, 1982 Tom was named associate senior vice chancellor for the health sciences.

Since his arrival at WPIC Tom had pushed vigorously to break down the walls between academic disciplines, thus fos-

tering interdisciplinary collaboration: "The Lone Ranger has died." One of his notable efforts was the establishment of a clinical and research program in geriatric medicine. Funded by a $1 million grant from Pittsburgh's Benedum Foundation it has gone on to secure $200 million in funding, making it the largest such program in the country.

Tom fixed on cancer treatment and research as a centerpiece and showpiece of interdisciplinary collaboration. He spread the net wide. Relations between Wes Posvar and Carnegie Mellon's president, Dick Cyert, perennially hovered between cool and frigid. As usual, the Detre charm worked its magic with Cyert; CMU was soon in for the Pittsburgh Cancer Institute (PCI), as well as a host of other collaborative efforts.

Two distinguished university clinical researchers, Bernard Fisher and Gerald Levey, were tapped by Tom to head the PCI planning committee. The final report was written by Jeff Romoff: ("I wrote it! I wrote every word of it!"). It called for the center to transcend all jurisdictions, assuring equal access for all hospitals, schools, and departments of both the University of Pittsburgh and CMU. Most importantly this plan again permitted Tom to "tax" clinical revenues of the participating hospitals. This assured a steady flow of funds that undergirded the effort to attract the best oncology researchers in the country.

Once again the ever helpful R. K. Mellon Foundation stepped up to the plate. It made an initial contribution of $3 million, followed up with an additional $3 million in 1986, and, again, a thumping $8 million in 1989. The Mellon family had supported the health sciences at the University of Pittsburgh before Tom Detre's arrival and would support it after his retirement. But during the Detre years (1973 to 1998) their belief in Tom's vision for the health sciences was a leading effort, both in terms of money and prestige. Time and time again Drew Mathieson, George Taber, and the Mellon

Brothers, Seward Prosser and Richard P., were with Tom every step of the way. Tom laid out his vision to these benefactors with charm and forceful logic.

The first candidate offered up by the search committee for the head of PCI was a specialist in chemotherapy protocols. He elicited a strong thumbs-down from Tom Detre. Tom likened chemotherapy treatments to the half-blind cartoon character Mr. Magoo, trying to swat flies with a sub-machine-gun. Chemotherapy has its place, but it did not represent the future of cancer treatment. PCI finally struck leadership pay dirt with an internationally recognized tumor immunologist from the National Cancer Institute, Ronald Herberman. Tom described him not as a man of steel but of "titanium." From 1985 until his retirement in 2009, Herberman built the Pittsburgh Cancer Institute into the nation's largest cancer center and home to over three hundred cancer-related faculty. While PCI is a standout example of interdisciplinary collaboration, it was but one of sixty such efforts begun during the Detre years. Among them are the AIDS Research Center, Biomedical Infomatics Center, the Tissue Engineering Initiative, and the Women's Heart Center.

As planned Nathan Stark announced his retirement in 1984, and a search committee headed by the distinguished surgeon Hank Bahnson recommended Detre to succeed him. Wes Posvar made the appointment in November. Not everybody was happy, but again Wes pushed it through. As Wes had changed his title from chancellor to president, Tom's new position was senior vice president for the health sciences. Tom immediately named Jeff Romoff associate vice president. The Detre/Romoff team now had a platform from which to pursue larger game.

UPMC was now clearly on the horizon. Let's interject some counterfactual history. Jeff Romoff is fatally injured by a bus while crossing 5th Avenue. Would there be a UPMC

today? Probably. Would it be today's path-breaking institution? Probably not.

The virtuous cycle of medical research, education, and unsurpassed patient care behind the WPIC success story was now to be applied to not just another department, hospital, or even a school. The vision of the Detre team—Detre, Romoff, John Paul, George Huber, and Loren Roth—was applied right across the entire spectrum, all the departments, all the schools, and eventually all the hospitals. It had taken ten years to transform WPIC. In less than half that time the architecture and mechanics for the transformation of the entire health system would be in place.

The University Health Center of Pittsburgh (UHCP) was established in 1965. The bricks and mortar were impressive. The UHCP hospitals included Presbyterian University, Eye & Ear, Montefiore, Veterans', Children's, Magee Women's, WPIC, and Falk Clinic. About all UHCP stood for was a loose grouping of independent teaching hospitals for the University of Pittsburgh. The hospitals and their boards and administrations jealously guarded their prerogatives of independence. However, the geography was favorable for synergies. With the exception of Magee Women's a few blocks away, all the other hospitals were set cheek by jowl on the upper campus. And while they were academic nonstarters and undermanaged, they were money makers with total revenues exceeding $400 million. But, at that time, no doubt the leading hospital in Pittsburgh was the tightly unified and aggressively managed Allegheny General on Pittsburgh's north side.

Not all the blame rested on the fiercely independent hospitals. The University School of Medicine paid the salaries of full-time faculty but received little return in the way of medical research and education. Past leadership had lacked either the vision or perhaps the intestinal fortitude to demand the kind of monetary support that was rightfully theirs.

How do you eat an elephant? One bite at a time. Falk Clinic, the outpatient clinic for Presbyterian University, was the first bite. It was a ripe apple ready to fall. The university's committee on the health sciences, chaired by Farrell Rubenstein, became the board at Falk and then brought it under the management of the Detre team. This action dovetailed nicely with the PCI initiative, as Falk provided outpatient care for PCI patients. This added to Tom Detre's "tax base," providing additional research funding.

For Tom Detre and his team, Presbyterian University was the "great white whale." But a frontal Captain Ahab assault (doubtless with Romoff throwing the harpoon) was not the way to go. Eye & Ear was the key by which to unlock the Golconda at Presbyterian. Eye & Ear Hospital occupied one hundred and eighty beds in the west wing of Presbyterian Hospital. With the recent advent of laser surgery for cataract operations, the procedure was done on an outpatient basis; thus Eye & Ear's beds were largely vacant. When Tom Starzl was recruited by Tom and Hank Bahnson to Pittsburgh, his revolutionary liver transplant program made Presbyterian the transplant capital of the world. Presbyterian was bursting at the seams and desperately needed those largely unoccupied beds in its own building, then controlled by Eye & Ear.

The logical move was for Presbyterian to take over Eye & Ear. Negotiations were under way, and it almost happened. Unfortunately for Presbyterian, but fortunately for the future of UPMC and the University of Health Sciences, the 800-pound gorilla pressed the smaller Eye & Ear too hard and finally the little guys turned down Presbyterian's offer at the last minute. J. Wray Connolly, a top H. J. Heinz executive who chaired the Eye & Ear board, called Tom Detre and suggested the university rather than Presbyterian should take over Eye & Ear.

For Tom and Jeff Romoff, the Eye & Ear opportunity was like manna from heaven. With Presbyterian salivating for

those one hundred and eighty vacant beds, Eye & Ear was a very strategic prize. But first there were a couple of wrinkles to be ironed out. Presbyterian Chair George Taber, their great Mellon benefactor, was none too happy about the Eye & Ear cup being dashed from his lips. But being every inch the gentleman, he knew that the Presbyterian board and administration had to share a good measure of the blame. Secondly Tom had to convince a risk-averse Pitt administration, in particular the chief business officer Jack Freeman, to accept the prize that had been offered. The price was a $10 million funding of the Eye & Ear Foundation. The $10 million was eventually generated by the efficiencies that the WPIC team wrung out of Eye & Ear. As well, the grants from the new Eye & Ear Foundation went to support the academic medical mission. The Eye & Ear key was now firmly in the Presbyterian lock.

Presbyterian Hospital, founded in 1893, opened its dominating edifice on Pitt's upper campus in 1938. It was a great building but not a great hospital. Presbyterian made no pretense of being an academic hospital; it was a self-proclaimed community hospital. The administration of Presbyterian sought to curry favor with Blue Cross, the insurance intermediary for Medicare, by keeping its reimbursement claims for Pitt's residency programs to a bare minimum. This ill-conceived "revenue minimization strategy" still left the hospital a solid earner but effectively killed any serious research effort at the university. The Presbyterian board was comfortable with its stewardship of a financially solid nonacademic teaching hospital. But Detre and Romoff were outraged because they knew from their WPIC experience that, with the holy trinity of superb patient care, education, and research, the hospital as well as the medical school could become institutions of national distinction.

Deep in their bones they knew this would happen. The Presbyterian board did not share this vision because they

didn't understand it. George Huber had a wonderful idea: "Let's educate the board." Detre, Romoff, and Huber interviewed all twenty-nine members of the Presbyterian board. George Taber was an able facilitator. Step by step the board was brought into the exciting vision of a great academic medical center.

As he did for Eye & Ear, Huber transformed a new shared vision into a working agreement in the 1986 "Concept Paper." Romoff called it the Magna Carta of UPMC. It established the Medical and Healthcare Division (MHCD—later UPMC) of the University of Pittsburgh, headed by Detre as president and Romoff as executive vice president. MHCD included WPIC, Falk Clinic, Presbyterian, and the recently merged Eye & Ear, as well as the School of Medicine. The WPIC model would in twenty years drive UPMC to national and international distinction.

Katherine Detre constantly badgered Tom about his smoking: "Only you and the truck drivers still smoke." Tom paid no mind and continued to puff away with an ebony cigarette holder at a three-pack-a-day rate. A heart attack in 1992 ended his smoking and altered his career. Romoff assumed responsibility for UPMC and Tom remained as the university's senior vice chancellor for the health sciences. Tom finally stepped down in 1998 in favor of Arthur Levine, a top director at the National Institute of Health. Tom Detre died in October 2010, at the age of eighty-six.

Today the results speak for themselves. For the fiscal year ending June 30, 2008, system-wide revenues for UPMC were $8,046,000. UPMC has twenty hospitals in Western Pennsylvania and expanding international operations in Italy, Ireland, the U.K., China, Colombia, and Japan. As of December 2008 the UPMC Health Plan insured 1,459,637 lives. Today UPMC is the largest academic medical center in the United States.

Hand in hand with the rise of UPMC goes Tom's transformation of the health sciences at the University of Pittsburgh. In fiscal 2009 the health sciences received NIH grants of $531 million, making the university the fifth largest recipient of NIH research funding. At the time of Tom's arrival, the university ranked thirty-seventh; when he stepped down in 1998 it stood tenth. He graciously allowed as how the move from tenth to sixth may have been more difficult than the long climb from thirty-seventh to tenth.

Dateline Pittsburgh—January 14, 2009. "Pitt scientists make key diabetes finding. A team led by Dr. Andrew F. Stewart, chief of the university's Division of Endocrinology and Metabolism, has identified key molecules." When you see these articles in local and national papers—and there have been hundreds in the past and there will be hundreds more in the future—think of Tom Detre. They are ongoing testimony to his enduring contributions to the region's mental, physical, and economic well-being.

12

AMERICAN GRIT: DICK SIMMONS

THE YEAR WAS 1900. A SIXTEEN-YEAR-OLD BOY, HIS parents, and three younger siblings passed through the long lines at Ellis Island. When the immigration officer stumbled over their difficult Russian name, he came up with a ready substitute, a good American name: Simmons. It was a new name for a new country in a new century. The young, freshly minted Joseph Simmons was Dick Simmons's father.

The family settled in as farmers in upstate New York. During the First World War Joseph moved off the farm and settled in Bridgeport, Connecticut. After a few years he scraped together the money to buy a service station. In 1920 he married Celia Kane who came to this country from Poland as a baby in 1902. Neither Joseph nor Celia had completed high school. They had three children: Bernard born in 1922, Rhoda in 1926, and, finally, Richard Paul Simmons in 1931.

Richard P. Simmons.

During the Depression Joseph almost lost his business. It provided the Simmons family with life's essentials, but that was about it. Life became more difficult for Dick when his dad had a heart attack in 1946. With the elder Simmons confined to bed rest, Dick spent days and weekends working at the service station. This cut into time for both study and extracurricular activities. Nevertheless, Dick managed to graduate second in his Bridgeport high school class of four hundred in 1949.

Math and science were Dick's favorite subjects, so an engineering career beckoned. One of Dick's teachers, taking a liking to him, asked him what he was going to do. Dick said: "I'm going to Rensselaer and study engineering." "Nothing

wrong with Rensselaer," his teacher said, "but why not go to the best: MIT?" Turning on a dime Dick applied to one college, Massachusetts Institute of Technology, and was accepted.

High school was easy for Dick; he was smart and he knew it. MIT was a whole new ballgame. There he competed against kids from the Bronx High School of Science, Peter Stuyvesant, and Brooklyn Tech. They gave the word "smart" a whole new meaning for Dick. He was the coxswain of the lightweight varsity crew and graduated north of the middle of his class. While his confidence in his intellectual capacities and his problem-solving skills remained intact, MIT taught him that he would not ride to success on a floodtide of brain power alone. Always a hard worker, Dick admits he never worked harder than he did at MIT.

His major at MIT was physical metallurgy. Early on he decided that his major would determine his choice of a career, and nowhere was metallurgy more important than in the steel industry. It is difficult to overestimate the size and stature of the U.S. steel industry in postwar America. The United States then possessed almost half of the world's steel capacity. All of the major steel producers were in the Fortune 100, and U.S. Steel and Bethlehem were in the top ten.

Dick received two job offers—from Inland Steel and Allegheny Ludlum. His advisor at MIT said: "Take the Allegheny offer. The metallurgy is more interesting." He might have added: "And more important in a specialty steel company." Starting at $338 a month in 1953, he became a titanium metallurgist and spent four years at Allegheny's flagship plant at Brackenridge, Pennsylvania. In 1957 he was sent to help build a titanium processing plant in Toronto, Ohio. Dick received a twofer for his time at Toronto. Moving through a succession of jobs at the plant gave him a keen taste for management. He also met his future wife Dottie Porter, whom he married in 1959; their two children, Brian and Amy, were born soon after.

That year Dick did something quite uncommon for a steel executive with a promising career; he quit. He told Dottie he intended to work for three companies and he did. His former boss at Brackenridge, Bob Eakin, had left Allegheny to become vice president of operations at family-owned Latrobe Steel. Dick asked him for a job and was immediately hired as manager of quality control. Dick logged three years at Latrobe and then Eakin got cross-wise with the controlling Saxman family and quit. Dick figured his lifespan at Latrobe was not too long. He then reached out to another of his Brackenridge bosses, Bob Henke, who was then general manager of Republic Steel's Central Alloy District in Canton, Ohio. Republic Steel was the third-largest steel company in the United States and the world's largest producer of bars and alloy products.

The Central Alloy District was an immense operation with two fully integrated steel plants employing over ten thousand people. It was far bigger than all of Allegheny Ludlum. Dick was named assistant to the general manager. It was an amorphous title, but it gave Dick a wide-ranging opportunity to leave his fingerprints all over the district. Bob Henke left and a Republic veteran, Herman Kaiser, was named as general manager. They asked Kaiser who he wanted as the assistant general manager (as distinguished from the more junior job of "assistant to"). Kaiser didn't bat an eyelash: "I want Dick Simmons." "You can't have Dick Simmons. He's too young." "Fine then. I don't want the job." He got Dick Simmons, who was then thirty-one.

Dick immediately set to work building the largest electric furnace melt shop in the world. Under normal circumstances the job was a killer, but it was compounded by labor and skilled trades competition from the immense General Motors project at Lordstown, Ohio. A smoker since the age of sixteen, Dick developed a perforated ulcer. Losing over half

his blood he came close to not making it. To top it all off, the culture at Republic was not conducive to Dick's intense and innovative management style. The company moved slowly and the big men who ran it (Republic seemed to hire them by the pound in those days) were content with its rather glacial pace.

Despite his near-death experience, Dick's work bringing up the huge melt shop at Canton attracted attention throughout the industry, and one who noticed was Roger Ahlbrandt, the newly named CEO at Allegheny Ludlum. He invited Dick back to Allegheny, first as vice president at the bar division and, within a year, as the vice president of manufacturing for the whole company.

In short order Dick stamped his mark on Allegheny with two bold initiatives. He moved the divisional structure from profit centers to cost centers on the premise that you could control costs but not selling prices. Second, at a considerable expense of time and money, he put in a comprehensive cost accounting system. Now for the first time Allegheny could determine the cost of its 150,000 products. Buttressed by his competence and intensity, initiatives like these catapulted Dick into the presidency of Allegheny Ludlum Steel in 1972 at the age of forty-one. He was the number three man in the company behind the CEO, Roger Ahlbrandt, and the newly hired chief operating officer, Bob Buckley.

Until 1970 Allegheny Ludlum was essentially a specialty steel company. Like other steel companies it took some tentative steps to diversify away from the low-margin steel business. With Allegheny and for the steel industry as a whole, these acquisitions were a matter of running away from the devil you did know into the arms of the devil you didn't know. With scant exception these diversification efforts were unsuccessful and in the case of Allegheny Ludlum (after 1980 Allegheny International) disastrous.

In 1971, Ahlbrandt and the board brought in Buckley to be the chief operating officer of the company and Roger's presumptive successor as CEO. A jowly lawyer, Buckley came with a very impressive track record at General Electric. He once remarked that his ascent through the ranks at GE had been so rapid that some people thought his last name was Electric. Jowly doesn't quite nail it for Bob Buckley. The Dick Tracy character Vitamin Flintheart brings us much closer to the mark.

Surprisingly, for two very strong-willed people, Buckley and Simmons got along quite well in the four years prior to Buckley's elevation to CEO in 1975. In fact, he was a critical part of the decision to elevate Dick to the presidency of the steel division. Despite a ramped-up acquisition pace, Buckley was supportive of Dick's efforts to modernize the steel business. Buckley was smart and aggressive. The BorgWarner Sheet Mill purchase is illustrative. Buckley: "Offer them $7.5 million, Dick." "Christ, Bob, the goddamned thing cost $30 million." "Try it."—they took it. BorgWarner never shipped more than eight hundred tons a month. Under Simmons's watchful eye, in three years the plant was shipping six thousand tons per month. It was a home run. The Buckley/Simmons honeymoon was still on, when in 1975 Dick was made senior vice president of the corporation and put on the board. Buckley told him: "You are my successor." Dick: "Not that I particularly believed him."

When Buckley sat down in the CEO's chair in 1975, it seemed as almost overnight he became a different person. It was apparent to both Roger Ahlbrandt and Dick—more airplanes, bigger airplanes, lavish off-site meetings more befitting a company ten times the size of Allegheny. Although capital funding continued to flow into the steel business, the Buckley style grated harshly against Dick's moral sensibilities. He soon became an unhappy camper, and, Dick being Dick, it showed.

As Buckley seemed intent upon becoming a conglomerate king—the next Royal Little or Henry Singleton—he soured on the steel business. It was slow growing, capital intensive, and labor intensive. It was everything the Boston Consulting Group told you you didn't want in a diversified portfolio. It had to go, and in its disposition Buckley could kill two birds with one stone. Along with the underperforming steel unit he could get rid of the annoying Simmons and his, euphemistically speaking, "plainspoken manner." Dick never bought into Buckley's vision for a new Allegheny. In 1978 he got his marching orders from Buckley: "Sell the business."

We must now back up a bit. In 1955, Bob Bozzone, a Rensselaer metallurgist, joined Allegheny Ludlum. He was assigned to the finishing plant at West Leechburg. The material that Leechburg finished was provided by Brackenridge, and Dick Simmons had immediate responsibility for the product received by Bozzone. A fifty-year friendship, one of the most notable and fruitful in the steel industry, was born out of a series of memos bouncing back and forth between the two—replete with charges and countercharges. Bozzone: "I can't produce a quality product out of this crappy steel you're sending me." Simmons: "The Brackenridge material is fine when it hits your door. You're screwing it up in your own operation." As they lived with some other Allegheny bachelors above a garage, they got the opportunity to go head to head over the issues. One evening Bob was coming back at 2:00 a.m. from a date with his future wife, Irene. He saw Simmons getting into his car: "Where are you going, Dick?" Dick: "Down to Brackenridge to a rolling to make sure your next shipment is *perfect*." Maybe Dick smiled—maybe he didn't.

They saw each other only intermittently during Dick's years at Latrobe and Republic. When Dick became vice president of manufacturing for the steel division, Bozzone, then production control manager at Leechburg, had high hopes

for a bigger job, either plant manager at Leechburg or production control manager for the entire division. On these hopes Bob rolled snake eyes. He told Dick: "I quit." In their years together Bob estimates he quit twice and was fired six times. Dick then summoned him to a "come to Jesus talk." Burning holes right through Bob's head he said: "You and I are going to run this company. Trust me." Bob trusted him, and they did end up running the company.

It was a remarkable relationship. Dick's laser-like intensity, coupled with an innate strategic sense, powered his path to success. Yet that very intensity and cocksure sense of the best course of action often didn't sit well with those on the receiving end. Bob, a gifted manager himself, was a superb people person. He would take an unpalatable directive from Dick, put a little spin on it, place his hand on the guy's shoulder, hit him with a hundred-watt smile, and the guy was ready to run out the door and execute Dick Simmons's directive to the letter. One of each was a perfect combination.

In selling the steel company, Dick was the point man on a project that soon looked like "mission impossible." He called in Bob Bozzone and told him he had to run the steel company while he traveled the world in search of a buyer. The United States, Canada, Japan, Europe, South Africa—steel companies, mining companies, and buyout shops including AEA Investors and Kohlberg Kravis & Roberts—no luck anywhere. Prospects were so bleak that Dick told Dottie that if the business didn't get sold he was leaving; he even took a couple of job interviews.

Meanwhile, Buckley turned up the heat. "If you don't sell it, I will, and you may not like the results." Unbeknownst to Dick, Buckley's alternative was the Miami raider Victor Posner. Compared to Posner, working for Buckley was like working for Jack Welch. Dick only became aware of the Posner option when Posner attempted to recruit Bob

Bozzone to run his Sharon Steel Company. Bob immediately went to Dick to tell him about his overtures and told him he would never work for Victor Posner—wouldn't even talk to him. Dick said: "Bob, go ahead and talk to him. We may not have jobs here."

Bob met with Posner in his Waldorf Towers suite in Manhattan. For openers, Bob was frisked to make sure he wasn't "packing." Victor was not a well-liked guy. Posner then appeared in a bathrobe surrounded by a covey of attractive young women—all with a common feature: "bedroom eyes." Bob was making $80,000 a year at the time and Victor opened with $140,000. After a series of noes on Bob's part, with the bidding up to $225,000, Posner quickly went from good cop to bad cop: "You're trying to rape me. I'll just buy Allegheny Ludlum and you'll be working for me for $140,000."

The dialogue went something like this: "But, Victor, aren't you at all concerned about the environmental problems?" Posner, his eyebrows popping up like window shades: "Environmental problems?" Bozzone: "I've got to tell you, Victor, honestly, because I like you. You're a nice guy. We've been dumping hexavalent chrome all over the melt yard for years. Dick and I have been praying that nobody would find out." Victor: "You've got to be shitting me. That son of a bitch Buckley never told me." Quite pleased with his performance, Bob couldn't wait to tell Dick the story.

In the late summer of 1980 a buyout opportunity surfaced in the person of Clint Murchison, the wealthy Texas oil man and owner of the Dallas Cowboys. More impressive to Dick than the Cowboys or the oil fortune was Clint's MIT affiliation as a graduate and trustee. "Why the hell does Murchison want to buy a goddamned steel company?" Dick: "I never wanted to ask that question. Okay?" Buckley wanted to get a deal done by December 26, 1980, the end of the newly renamed Allegheny International's fiscal year. He set a

reasonable price: book value of $195 million plus assumption of debt and pension liabilities. Dick never quibbled with the price. But at a prime rate of 20 percent he negotiated hard for better terms.

Soon after Murchison surfaced Dick engaged Chuck Queenan, the managing partner of Kirkpatrick & Lockhart, to represent the management buyout group. As subsequent events proved out, it was one of the best decisions Dick ever made. Chuck and Dick then recruited Tom Bigley, the managing partner of Ernst & Ernst on the accounting side. The price was reasonable, and the other terms were very reasonable. All the press reports cited a cash payment of $65 million. It was never $65 million; it was always $20 million in cash. Murchison was to put up $19 million, $15 million in preferred stock and $4 million in common. Dick and his sixteen-member management group put up $1 million in common, so the management group had 20 percent of the equity for $1 million. Murchison for his $19 million had 80 percent. The remaining $175 million came from Allegheny International and a bank syndicate in the form of preferred stock, subordinated debt, and term debt.

In early November it looked like a smooth close on December 26, 1980. Then the deal started to change. Murchison's deal man, John Jones, suggested that perhaps they could do the deal with less than $19 million or perhaps with no equity at all. Whether the ultrarich Murchison was temporarily cash strapped or whether he thought he could negotiate a much better deal, $19 million no longer seemed to be on the table.

Dick still wanted to do the deal with Murchison, but he was becoming increasingly uneasy about his interactions with Jones. Things were soon brought to a head when Queenan and Bigley told Dick that, if he went ahead with Murchison, they could no longer represent the company. Dick needed

little convincing. When word reached Dallas that the deal was floundering, Murchison himself made a rare trip to Pittsburgh in an attempt to right things with his CEO-to-be. In patented Simmons style, Murchison got a one-two punch. He had to come up with precisely $19 million cash, not one dollar less, and Jones had to be off the deal. This was not acceptable to Murchison, and, while he still wanted to do the deal, it appeared unlikely that Simmons would be part of it. They now headed on separate but parallel paths to the closing scheduled for December 26.

Needless to say, Buckley wasn't a happy camper when he was informed that Dick would not do the deal with Murchison. As if Dick needed any more pressure on him at this time, Buckley told him: "No deal and you're fired." Dick said he intended to find another buyer. All this was through intermediaries as Dick and Buckley were no longer on speaking terms.

Dick then turned to Queenan: "Find me somebody else." Queenan: "Dick, I'm not an investment banker. That's what they're used for." This request was both impractical and somewhat unreasonable. With closing only three weeks away and a deal already negotiated, the odds of finding a new investor for this major, complex transaction were hovering between slim and none. And then in this Christmas season, first the worst and then the best of times for Dick Simmons, a wonderful thing happened; it was pure serendipity. Chuck Queenan pulled a $19 million rabbit out of the hat. Its name was George.

George Tippins was a Yale-educated engineer who had taken his father's small used equipment business and pushed it into the top ranks of steel rolling mill manufacturers. He had recently delivered a highly profitable hot strip mill to the Pohang Iron & Steel Company (Posco), the South Korean steel company emerging as one of the world's giants. Chuck Queenan had been his attorney and advisor for years.

George had a problem. From the Posco contract and others, he had over $25 million in a company bank account. If he doesn't distribute the cash in dividends, he is subject to an excess accumulation penalty tax of 70 percent. If he distributes it as dividends they are taxed at 70 percent. Either way he's going to have to write a check to Uncle Sam for $20 million. But, if George made an investment in a related business, he would not have to pay the penalty tax or dividend it out—no check to Uncle Sam. In philosophical terms the Allegheny opportunity was an "elegant solution."

Queenan presented it to George Tippins. He didn't mince words. The deal was already negotiated down to the last comma and semicolon. In fact a definitive agreement had been drafted by Allegheny and the Simmons group. The only change was substituting Tippins's signature for that of Murchison. George liked the deal for two reasons. First and foremost 70 percent of the $19 million he put up was "found money," courtesy of the United States government. His effective outlay was $6.4 million for 80 percent of a company with $600 million in revenue. George was a "motivated" buyer. Secondly, he rather liked the idea of owning Allegheny Ludlum. With the stroke of the pen he went from being a successful used equipment builder to an industrial statesman.

Chuck Queenan put Simmons and Tippins together. George was a tough enough guy—the equipment business is a tough business. But he didn't wear it on his sleeve. They got along well. Tippins had the dough; that was enough for Dick. George then made the best business call of his life, betting that the tough little guy looking him right in the eye could steer Allegheny through a lousy steel market and rough financial seas, whipped by a 20 percent prime interest rate. On December 19, one week before the closing, Tippins agreed to proceed.

But now Dick and his new partner George Tippins had to surmount one final hurdle. Bob Buckley had two options: Murchison and Tippins. The image-conscious Buckley naturally preferred Murchison, the owner of the Dallas Cowboys, to a used equipment dealer. And by this time even the mention of the name Simmons sent a sharp pain coursing through Buckley's ample midsection.

Dick knew that Buckley would sell the deal out from under him. In concert with Chuck Queenan and Bob Bozzone, Dick devised a plan to thwart a possible sale to Murchison. Dick and Bob asked each member of the sixteen-man management group to be prepared to resign. They believed in Dick and followed him to a man. On December 26 Murchison might have owned a steel company, but he would have no management team to run it. In retrospect both he and Bob Bozzone believe this is what killed the Murchison option.

The moment of truth finally came on December 26 in the offices of Buchanan Ingersoll (Allegheny's attorneys) in the U.S. Steel building. Murchison had a team of attorneys in town. Nobody knew if they would show up. Chuck Queenan had K&L prepare two sets of closing documents—one for Murchison and one for Tippins. The Murchison team never showed. The drama was over, but the humor wasn't.

George Tippins came prepared for a high-stakes poker game as well as a closing. He had with him not one check for $19 million, but several checks to be used as poker chips: a red one for $10 million, a blue one for $5 million, and four little yellow ones for $1 million each. With various combinations of the six checks you could get any amount from $1 million to $19 million. It was quite ingenious. George intended to negotiate on the spot with Buckley. Excepting George this left everybody else in the crowded room a little slack jawed. Queenan: "I had to take him out of the room a couple of

times." The deal closed for $19 million. It is hard to overstate the contribution Chuck Queenan made to the Allegheny Ludlum buyout—in all likelihood, no Queenan, no deal.

Dick and Chuck then hot-footed it down to the Duquesne Club to report to a very anxious management team. Right in front of the Alcoa building Dick stepped in a pothole and sprained his ankle. He hobbled into the room and Bozzone said: "Dick, I didn't know closings were that tough."

Life was good under George Tippins as the 80 percent owner of Allegheny Ludlum, but the external environment was very difficult. Inflation was raging, the prime rate was 21 percent, and there were some bankruptcies in the steel industry. Margins were under pressure in 1982, but in 1984 the company posted record sales of $763 million and earnings of $36.4 million in 1984. The capital program initiated under Allegheny International was beginning to pay big dividends.

Tippins's interference was minimal. He did nudge Allegheny Ludlum to buy an annealing line from his equipment company. On occasion he asked permission to use the Allegheny Ludlum suite at the Duquesne Club, and he did spend one sunny Christmas afternoon pumping fifty-caliber slugs from his new machine gun into the slag pile at Brackenridge. His wife Carolyn got a bonus. She was driving their children to school in a beat-up station wagon with a bad muffler—had to keep the windows down. "I didn't know he had $20 million. I'm going to buy a new car."

In late 1986 Dick and George agreed that it made sense for the management group to buy him out. The negotiations took about five minutes. Dick offered book value at $375 a share. George pointed out that his stock was control stock and suggested $400 a share. Dick agreed. This transaction gave George $190 million, or a ten times return on his initial $19 million investment. If we use his tax-advantaged cost basis

of $6.4 million, it was thirty times. Far bigger payouts for the management group were yet to come.

But first Dick had to find a mountain of debt to finance the transaction. PNC, as their agent bank, put together a debt syndicate of $381 million against a nominal Allegheny Ludlum net worth of $19 million. It was like balancing a basketball on a pencil. In the end, the ever-helpful Tippins agreed to take back $50 million of the paper. Dick also bought back the preferred from the then–cash strapped Allegheny International at a deep discount. The Tippins buyout was completed by December of 1986—exactly six years after the original LBO.

Dick Simmons has often said he is the luckiest man in the world. Lightening struck again on May 8, 1987 when the initial public offering window opened briefly and Allegheny Ludlum's investment banker, Goldman Sachs, was able to take the company public—22 million shares were issued at $25 per share. They opened on the New York Stock Exchange at $27.50, giving the company a market capitalization of $605 million. Management held 71 percent of the shares. During the initial buyout, Dick had allocated shares amongst the sixteen top managers. Management participation was unusually broad. Dick put up $325,000 and Bob Bozzone $160,000. The senior officers were given $50,000, and the rest $25,000 allocations. The return to Dick and his team upon the IPO was 671 to 1 times invested capital. Dick's original $325,000 turned into $218 million. To put this in perspective, the venture returns to Kleiner Perkins and Sequoia on Google—the most lucrative venture deal ever—were a paltry 300 to 1. And as Allegheny's stock value appreciated over the next decade the returns more than doubled. An instant member of the Forbes 400, Dick Simmons was the fastest "rich Pittsburgher" ever.

He also made significant contributions in both time and money to the Pittsburgh community. He served as chairman

of the Allegheny Conference and on several other boards. Most notable was his tireless devotion to the Pittsburgh Symphony. In addition to serving twice as board chair, he supported two capital campaigns, the first for $5 million and the second for a whopping $29.5 million. MIT, CMU, Pitt, and Washington & Jefferson have been the beneficiaries of his largesse through grants and scholarships for Western Pennsylvania students.

Dick teaches a class at Carnegie Mellon's Tepper School. He will ask the class: "How many of you are ethical?" Like a rocket barrage every hand fires into the air. Dick bounces back: "You never know until you look the tiger in the eye." In his fifty-year career Dick has looked several tigers in the eye. In 1980 he walked away from the opportunity of a lifetime with the Murchison buyout. In this decade he faced another ferocious tiger labeled "intestinal fortitude." In 1999 Dick's holdings in Allegheny Technologies were worth well over $400 million. With bankruptcy a possibility in 2002, the stock dropped to below $3 a share. His holdings were then less than $20 million. He never sold a share until the stock rebounded to over $50. There is more than one way to look a tiger in the eye.